OUTDOOR COOKING

ARIZONA
HIGHWAYS BOOK

TEXT BY LOUISE DEWALD
EDITED BY ROBERT C. DYER

COLOR PHOTOGRAPHY: RICHARD EMBERY   PHOTOGRAPHIC FOOD STYLIST: PAMELA RHOADS EMBERY

Grill Time

Time on the grill varies according to size and shape of the meat. These guidelines are approximate, for a nonwindy day, medium-hot coals.

Beef: Hamburgers, 4 to 6 inches above coals — rare, 3 minutes on first side, 4 minutes on second; well-done, 3 minutes on first side, 12 minutes on second. Steak, 1 1/2 to 2 inches thick — rare, 4 to 5 minutes on first side, 8 on second; well-done, 4 to 5 minutes on first side, 12 to 15 on second.

Chicken: Halves and parts, 4 to 5 inches above coals. Dark meat, 30 minutes, basting and turning. White meat, 20 minutes, basting and turning. Do not baste the last 5 minutes. Done when juices run clear.

Fish: Oil the grid, fish basket, and fish. If cooking on the grill, wrap fish in foil. Measure at thickest point and cook 15 minutes per inch. Done when a fork can flake opaque flesh, not transparent.

Lamb & Veal: Oil grids, place 4 to 5 inches above coals. Chops, 1 inch thick, 7 to 8 minutes per side. Shanks, best marinated overnight before grilling.

Pork: Cook over medium to low heat; chops until interior turns white, roast until interior temperature of 160 degrees F.

(FRONT COVER) *The barbecue grill, the cooker of choice for most Arizonans who head for the outdoors — even if no further than the backyard patio. A hand-held grill basket holds a variety of fresh vegetables, along with mushrooms, as glowing coals impart a flavor that simply cannot be matched on the kitchen range.*

(TITLE PAGE) *Juicy cubes of lamb interspersed with colorful vegetables create the shish kebab — an all-time favorite of outdoor chefs. Beef, pork, chicken, shrimp, or other meat, fish, or fowl, may be substituted for lamb. The result is a dining delight, whether in campground or backyard.*

Measuring Up

A shake	1/8 teaspoon
A pinch	1/8 to 1/4 teaspoon
A canteen capful	A slurp; less than a teaspoon
1 tablespoon	3 teaspoons
2 tablespoons	1 liquid ounce
4 tablespoons	1/4 cup
8 ounces	1 cup
2 cups	1 pint (16 ounces)
4 cups	1 quart
4 quarts	1 gallon, minimum liquid for a day's hike

Arizona Highways Heritage Cookbook and other books about Arizona and the Southwest are available through *Arizona Highways*.
For a free catalog, call toll-free nation-wide 1-800-543-5432 (Phoenix area, 258-1000), or write *Arizona Highways* at 2039 West Lewis Avenue, Phoenix, Arizona 85009-2893.

CONTENTS

Introduction 4-7

Chapter **1** Cooking Methods & Fires 8-11

Chapter **2** Breakfast All Day 12-27

Chapter **3** Game, Meat, & Barbecue 28-41

Chapter **4** Fish & Fowl 42-59

Chapter **5** Vegetating 60-69

Chapter **6** Fruitables 70-77

Chapter **7** Sauces, Marinades, & Zappers 78-91

Chapter **8** Flour Power 92-105

Chapter **9** Dessert Me-Please! 106-119

Chapter **10** Quenchers 120-135

Chapter **11** For the Fun of It 136-143

Chapter **12** While You Wait 144-153

Chapter **13** S'mores 154-167

Glossary.....168-169 Index.....170-173 Acknowledgments.....175

Outdoor Cooking: From Backyard to Backpack

Prepared by the Related Products Section of *Arizona Highways* magazine, a monthly publication of the Arizona Department of Transportation. Hugh Harelson - Publisher / Wesley Holden - Managing Editor / Robert J. Farrell - Associate Editor

Copyright 1991 By the Department of Transportation, State of Arizona. All rights reserved. Printed in Japan. No part of this book may be reproduced in any form or by any means without permission of *Arizona Highways*, 2039 W. Lewis Avenue, Phoenix, Arizona 85009.

Library of Congress Catalog Number 91-70843
ISBN 0-916179-32-X

Introduction

Outdoor Cooking leads you through outdoor cookery, grub to gourmet, portraying in food a trailway of Arizona's cultural culinary differences. Here are recipes for zesty food to be cooked and eaten outside, with go-alongs to cook inside. Gorp to cobblers, squash to steak, here is documentation of Arizona's vigor. Life can be a picnic — morning, noon, or night.

Much of what was very old is new again, updated with spiced marinades and sauces. As fresh as a whiff of mesquite smoke, here you will find recipes for game on a stick, Indian stews, and hearty cowboy cooking beefed and beaned. Today, however, chuck wagon cooking may mean a tailgate buffet. From backpack to barbecue, each form of cooking mirrors a lifestyle endorsed in this state — Scout and Campfire kids' cookery, lake and river pack food, hike and bike quick food, starlight patio parties, and a raft of picnics.

Somewhere within most of us is a sense of past communal cooking that feeds the fires of outdoor cooking. All food was once outdoor food. The oldest form of cookery is what we now call trail food. In prehistoric Arizona, they made do "on the trail" with mesquite beans, prickly pear cactus fruit, and selected wild greens. Then some early hunter-gatherer dared to try game that had been cooked by wild range fire. It was the tantalizing aroma, no doubt, that gave him the courage to snatch a bite. Today, guests at a contemporary pig pickin' pull slow-roasted meat from bones in much the same manner.

(OPPOSITE PAGE) *Outdoor cooking is for everyone — even those who never leave home. Nearly every backyard, patio, or balcony is made complete by some kind of cooker — built-in or portable; gas, electric, or charcoal; open coals or smoke. The results are good food, and good company.*

Over the centuries, mankind has advanced from range fire-seared meat, to roasting food on a stick, to cooking in clay pots. Barbecuing is believed to have originated with the Indians of the Caribbean, who smoke-dried meat on woven green wood strips over slow coals. The Spanish dropped anchor to chat, liked it, adopted it, and named it *barbacoa*. They took the idea to Mexico, added their own distinctive touches, and barbecue became a Southwestern specialty.

Chuck wagon cooking began during the era of great trail drives following the Civil War. Without those outdoor kitchens and range cooks, the cattle industry would not have developed so successfully, and the world would have been deprived of that still-familiar summons, "Come an' get it!" Dude ranches and resorts used chuck wagons until the majority of their guests chose golf carts over horses.

Outdoor eating is so basic to our genes and so conducive to a feeling of pleasure that Americans have made it a $6-billion-a-year business. Arizona is a natural for this outdoor cooking boom. If ever a spot on earth, by birth, breeding, and choice, was created for the fresh-air cook, Arizona is it. With more than 11 million acres of national forest land, and numerous lakes and trout streams, Arizona's outdoors is a guest room for much of its growing population.

Recipes say it all. Consider the staff-of-life, bread. Arizona's breads range from freckled circles of corn and wheat tortillas, to blue corn piki, golden puffs of fry bread, iron-skillet cornbread, Dutch-oven biscuits, and the sweet mystery of sourdough. I call these story-

(LEFT) *Outdoor cooking made the West, and still defines it. Time-tested ingredients include barbecued ribs, cowboy beans, camp biscuits, roasted corn, and a sweet finisher — in this case, a dried apple turnover.*

telling breads — put together with little yarns for those who come new to the campfire.

Fires, too, are a story. Until the 1940s, those who cooked over open fires were mostly pioneers, Scouting types, or hobos. Almost overnight, so it seemed, the general population began charcoal broiling in the backyard. That marked the zenith of our love affair with meats. Spit roasting, grilling, smoking, and barbecuing took to charcoal with a passion.

Traditionally, barbecues, from giant pits to open grills, have been found on the ranch. Modern outdoor cooking is much different. The camp stove and small charcoal grill are a must. Large cooking fires often are prohibited due to fire danger and sheer numbers of camp cooks. Backpacker principles, of necessity, are "pack it in, keep it light, pack it out." River runners established themselves as gourmet beach chefs. Picnics have gone from the Renoir-style eating affairs, to all-day-luncheons-on-the-ground, to

patio dress-up for dinner bashes. And while some outdoor, camping, hiking, and trail food became more selective, home grilling went gourmet.

I always knew the scope of outdoor food was as limitless as Arizona's hours of sunshine. Still, I was unprepared for the bonanza of outdoor recipes uncovered as I researched this cookbook. Psychologists have been making a big deal out of the return to "comfort foods"— meat loaf, stews, cobblers, and such. Yet maybe, just maybe, outdoor cooking is the ultimate way to prepare and enjoy comfort food. It was, and surely still is, a way of life.

— *Louise DeWald*

(RIGHT) Red Mountain, east of Mesa, is the scenic backdrop for an upscale, springtime, tailgate picnic on the desert. The cake and green chile pie are definite "take-alongs," but chicken can easily be grilled on the spot, guaranteeing tantalizing aromas from the cooking fire.

Cooking Methods & Fires

This book is written for outdoor cooks of every skill level, including beginners. Some methods and recipes can be used as shortcuts, but this is not a fast-food book. Cooking is the message.

When I was a Girl Scout, our intrepid leader, Laura Brass, taught us all we needed to know about fires — how to build a fire; how to light a fire; how to fight and douse a fire.

Today, fire is not merely fire. First, choose your type: pit, grill, smoker, spit, outside fireplace. Then your fuel: wood chunks or chips, charcoal or briquets, propane or natural gas, kerosene, or electric. The test of fire is the taste.

Most outdoor cooks begin their at-home education with a simple grill and a bag of either charcoal or briquets. What's the difference between one black lump and another?

Charcoal came first and is still the preference of gourmet and professional grillers. It is made from hardwood, no additives or fillers, just burned chunks of mesquite, oak, hickory, or fruit woods. It burns clean and hot and has a low ash content. Charcoal is reusable if removed and cooled with water as soon as the meal is served (after second helpings, of course).

(OPPOSITE PAGE) *Flames flickering from burning briquets mean that cooking time is approaching. When flames die down, and a fine gray ash coats the briquets, the food goes on, and the outdoor chef's skills come into full play.*

Briquets were devised by Henry Ford as a by-product of wood alcohol. The barbecue boom of the 1950s transferred the briquet into the home cooking market, where it has become a popular fuel. Briquets are a combination of hardwood charcoal, anthracite coal, and such surprising beginnings as peach and apricot pits. Some cooks reject coal briquets, claiming they leave an aftertaste.

Briquets have the edge over charcoal when it comes to the amount of time it takes to burn off to the gray ash cooking stage. This is important to those who get agonizing hunger pangs the minute the fire is lit. Grill experts advise that briquets light faster because of a chemical additive. To avoid the taste that tells, care must be taken not to put food over their coals until gray ash covers the surface. One-step "easy-lighting" briquets are pledged to be grill-ready in 20 minutes.

Until you find what's best suited to your needs, expect a few slow fire starts. At the point of frustration, refrain from drenching the charcoal with lighter fluid unless you enjoy the taste of it. Also, be careful; liquid starters can be dangerous.

The safest fire starters are "easy-lighting briquets," wood kindling, an electric starter, or the "kindle can."

Although wet wood is the last thing normally desired for a fire, wood chips extend that smoky, taste-of-the-wild flavor when soaked and tossed over glowing coals. Cover the meat and fire at once and the resulting smoke will permeate whatever is grilling, adding your choice of apple, olive, hickory, or mesquite for extra flavor. Don't overdo the amount or you'll put out the fire.

First, you work to make a fire. Then wait for coals. Next, as the food cooks, extinguish flare-ups caused by fat and meat juices dripping onto hot coals with a squirt bottle.

At the same time, you may be dry-mopping or

Round or rectangular, pie irons provide camp cooks with a maximum of menu variety with a minimum of cleanup.

basting and, for further flavor, sprinkling water-soaked herbs on the coals. Now you're beginning to understand why barbecue chefs "trim" or "correct the seasoning."

Charcoal and wood are not the only source of fire — especially at home. In our relentless search for a faster, better way, Americans took to the gas grill until today it has taken on the role of an outdoor kitchen appliance. The Sun Belt's lifestyle has placed a grill on almost every patio, with charcoal slipping in use and gas growing. Gas grill owners agree that speedier heat-up time and absence of ashes to clean are major reasons. Built-in, on wheels, or on a pedestal, they are basically stove-like.

Gas feeds in from a permanent natural gas hookup or a refillable tank of liquid propane. *Never use one kind of fuel in a grill meant for the other.*

Gas flames are adjusted through burners by stove-type controls. Above the burners may be a heat distributor of natural lava rock and a cast-iron grate, or the newer ceramic or pumice "briquets," metal bar grids, or solid metal plates with a stainless steel grate.

Experts say food from a gas grill tastes best when cooked with the cover down. (Gas loses heat quickly when the lid is up.) Think of gas cooking as oven-style. You can still use wood chips for mesquite mystique or other smoky flavor. Cooking tools are the same. Both charcoal and gas camps claim a far superior product when the smoke clears and taste is the judge.

However you grill, be aware of recommendations made by some health specialists: first microwave meat for a minute or two, then toss out the juice in which potential carcinogens collect. Grilling over moderate heat to rare or medium, rather than well done, also lowers the risk.

◆ Fuels & Tools ◆

FOR THE FIRE

An old oven grate (not a refrigerator rack)
Covered cooker; grill that can roast, smoke, or steam
Dutch oven; cast iron pots for buried-in-coals cooking and baking
Fire chimney or kindle can
Folding portable grill
Fire bowl on legs or spit
Griddles, long-handled
Gas stoves and grills
Hibachi
Smokers; water smokers double as braziers without water

FOR THE COOK

Asbestos mitts
Baskets, adjustable for grill or spit
Foil, heavy-duty, for cooking and covering
Basting mop or brush (paintbrush will do)
Water bottle, sprinkler, or pump spray for flare-ups
Drip pans
Forks, long-handled and sturdy
Knives, best possible,
Spatula, long-handled
Iron skillets
Tongs, two pairs; one for coals, one for food
Skewers
String, soaked in water
Trivets, racks, rotisserie, and attachments
Meat thermometer

◆

Before buying fire equipment, consider where and what you'll be cooking.
The portable is fine for appetizers, shrimp, hot dogs, and burgers. The large,
covered grill is worth the expense for year-round outdoor cuisine.

Breakfast All Day

Some folks can't wait to get up and eat breakfast. Others shudder at the thought, and require coffee brought to their beds or sleeping bags. Brunch starts late and extends breakfast to buffet.

I once did a magazine story about what people eat for breakfast. Erma Bombeck said, "Flour. Anything with flour." Rex Allen said, "Steak." Radio host Pat McMahon said, "Vitamins and ice cream." Bruce Babbitt, then governor of Arizona, said he ate light at home except on Sundays; heavy on the road, when breakfast usually included a conference, or when hiking, for stamina.

Most of us eat that way — according to the moment. And a lightly breezed patio or a dew-drenched, sparkling morning perks the appetite. Fresh air and freedom send a message.

Breakfast is such a comfortable, friendly meal when it is allowed to proceed at its own pace that we can scramble it, flip it, sausage it, or granola and juice it any time of day. This chapter offers such recipes.

(OPPOSITE PAGE) *On a crisp morning in a pine forest, with a mountain brook gurgling in the background, there's no such thing as a delicate appetite, and a rib-stickin' breakfast includes sausage, eggs, Dutch oven biscuits, and camp coffee. Of course, the cook with flair can turn out more surprising fare, chosen from this chapter.*

Chigger Flats Scramble

The name says a lot. This is perfect for a fishing or hiking meal when the chiggers make you scramble — and it's hearty enough to get you to Chigger Flats (near Payson). Helen Foster collected outdoor recipes in more than 20 years of working at *Arizona Highways*.

Cook 4 slices bacon until crisp. Drain on paper. Reserve 2 tablespoons drippings and lightly brown a drained No. 2 can of hominy. Beat together 4 eggs with salt and pepper to taste. Add to hominy. Cook until just set, stirring lightly. Top with favorite grated cheese and crumbled bacon. Serves four to six, ready to go!

Bogota Bread Omelet

Clemencia and Mario Tafur grew up in Bogota, Colombia, meeting when he was in medical school. Both loved cooking and attended Julia Child classes after they came to the States. Still, a bit of home is welcome, especially when put together by son Mario Jr., for sunshine breakfast in their Paradise Valley garden.

4 slices white bread, cubed
1/2 cup milk
3 eggs, well beaten
1/2 teaspoon sugar
2 tablespoons cooking oil

Place the bread and milk in shallow, heat-resistant casserole or heavy metal pan that has been coated with the oil. Wait until the bread has completely soaked up the milk. Beat eggs with sugar and pour over bread. Place cooking grill 4 to 6 inches above bed of medium-glowing coals. Make a tent of foil to enclose omelet. Cook 12 to 14 minutes and check. When tester comes out clean, slice into wedges and serve with marmalade or syrup and mounds of fresh fruit. Serves six.

The Incredible Egg

The incredible, edible egg was first hatched and eaten outdoors. On this continent it remains an all-day favorite, starring in a dozen varied roles for breakfast and brunch. Susan Lacy of Scottsdale, who has represented the American Egg Board, considers the omelet a perfect patio entree. "I've taught hundreds of home cooks how to make an omelet the easy way." She advises, "Let your guests do it. Put out the eggs and diced cheeses, fresh mushrooms and peppers, cooked chicken or crab. It adds up to a healthy, hearty breakfast, lunch, or dinner."

On the road or trail, eggs travel best in protective plastic cartons or when broken into a plastic jar. Cradle them in your pack — but not too close to your back. Body heat can cause spoilage, and nobody wants a rotten egg. Scrambled, they tuck happily into pita bread.

For Mole-in-the-Hole, bite the center out of a heavy slice of bread and drop in the frying pan. Melt a little butter in the pan, plop the egg in the hole, scatter bacon bits or shredded cheese and a splash of salsa over Mole and cook 2 minutes. Cover if you like your egg yolk cloudy.

As for dried eggs: Add bits of green onion, squash, tomato, and cheese, and eat fast, saying, "Lots of power protein down the hatch." It's true. By some magic, powdered eggs have *more* protein than fresh — and they don't break.

The Great Bean Sprout Omelet

From her home base in Globe, Betty Jean Faris taught cooking with zest for University of Arizona Extension Services. She was for omelets, any time, any meal. "Lots of home cooks are scared to death of omelets," she says. "Just beat the devil out of the eggs with a beater." And, contrary to other recipes, she advises, "never use milk. You need water for steam. For crunch and nutrition, add sprouts and fresh parsley, tossed in toward the end."

2 eggs
2 tablespoons water
Salt and pepper
1/2 tablespoon butter
1/2 to 1 cup alfalfa, soy, lentil, or mung
  bean sprouts
1 tablespoon chopped, fresh parsley

Combine eggs, water, salt, and pepper, and beat. Heat omelet pan or small fry pan with sides that curve, add butter, and spread around. Add egg mixture. Immediately lift egg mixture which has cooked, and allow uncooked egg mixture to come in contact with hot pan. Sprinkle sprouts and parsley on one-half the omelet. Fold over and tip onto warm serving plate.

Never hesitate with an omelet. This is one serving. Most omelets are made one at a time, ingredients added according to personal choice. Eggstra-ordinary for the outside camp or patio cook.

Machaca and Eggs

Artist and writer Kathy McRaine gathered ranch recipes for years, then bunched 'em into a volume called *Cow Country Cuisine*. Dr. Roy Rodriguez gave her the best eggs and Mexican dried beef recipe I've tasted — a great energizer any time of day. It's a cinch to cook in an iron skillet over low coals.

Carne Machaca (for the recipe see the *Arizona Highways Heritage Cookbook*), which means "battered meat" in Spanish, originally was the term for a method in which *carne seca* (dried meat) was made more chewable, a matter of pounding with stones, then adding chiles, onion, and lime juice. Fellow Tucsonans Ray and Sheri Holbrook collaborated with Dr. Rodriguez on this spunky treasure.

2 cups machaca
2 or 3 tablespoons oil
1 onion, sliced thin
2 green chiles, roasted and diced,
  or one 4-ounce can
1 large chopped tomato
1/2 bottle beer, Mexican preferred
Scrambled eggs, 4 to 6

Sauté the machaca, onion, chiles, and tomato in the oil, moistening with the beer. Simmer about 15 minutes until vegetables are soft. Serve with eggs, salsa, and gorditas (little thick corn cakes), or flour tortillas.

Asian Omelet

Grace B. Rodier, of Scottsdale, spent her early married life in China and the Philippines. Douglas MacArthur, Dwight Eisenhower, and "Vinegar Joe" Stilwell became her friends. The same simple after-concert dish they enjoyed became a favorite light brunch specialty of her Scottsdale sorority sisters. Gracie stirred this up in minutes, big skillet on a hibachi, under a bower of grapevines. Vary with chicken or pork.

1 cup shelled shrimp
1 cup diced ham
3 to 4 cups cooked rice
4 green onions, finely sliced, with tops
1 tablespoon soy sauce or more, to taste
2 large eggs, beaten lightly

Dice shrimp and ham and brown slowly in bits of ham fat, if any, or rice oil. Add onions and stir in soy sauce, as rice is combined with shrimp and ham. When hot, pour beaten eggs over all. Cover just 2 minutes, heat lowered. Egg acts as a tender binder. Serve at once with more soy sauce for those who want it, and side dishes of litchi nuts and mandarin oranges. Serves three or four.

Sunrise Brunch Strata

Everything But the Ants, a painstakingly complete picnic cookbook by the Phoenix Junior League, contains this cheese strata. Assembled a day ahead, it's ideal for any brunch or supper. Lisa Pierson, the book's recipe tester, suggests champagne daisies, citrus cups, and croissants, followed by coffee cake and Kahlúa coffee, followed by streams of ants.

12 slices bread
2 cups ham, diced
10-ounce package chopped broccoli, cooked and drained
3/4 pound sharp cheese, grated
6 slightly beaten eggs
3 1/2 cups milk
2 tablespoons minced onion
1/2 teaspoon salt
1/4 teaspoon dry mustard
1/4 pound sharp cheese, grated

Use cookie cutter to cut center from each piece of bread. Cut remaining bread into cubes. Layer the cubes on the bottom of a 13 by 9 by 2-inch pan. Layer on ham, broccoli, and 3/4 pound cheese. Cover with bread rounds. Combine eggs, milk, onion, and seasonings, and pour over all. Refrigerate, covered, 12 hours or overnight. Bake, uncovered, at 350 degrees for 55 minutes. Sprinkle with additional 1/4 pound cheese the last 5 minutes. Let stand 10 minutes before serving or before wrapping in aluminum foil and newspapers to take to picnic. This wrapping maintains heat in safety an hour; it will remain safe longer on coolish days. Serves eight to 10 persons; the ants wait for dessert.

All-purpose Salsa

This *salsa cruda* (raw) wonder was the most popular salsa recipe I put in print during 24 years of writing. Ruth Ann Kennedy-Iwai and her mother, Beth, assured me: "It can't be beaten for dips. It is a wonderful taco sauce. We particularly like it flour-thickened and cooked with meat for a really great chile burro." All true. And it's magic on eggs.

　1 small onion
　1 fresh green chile pepper
　1 fresh jalapeño pepper
　4 sprigs fresh cilantro
　16-ounce can tomatoes with juice
　1 fresh tomato
　1 tablespoon salt, optional

Chop all ingredients, and mix well but lightly. Recipe makes 1 quart. Keep in refrigerator, then hustle it front row for any outdoor meal.

Notes

_____
_____
_____
_____
_____
_____
_____
_____
_____
_____
_____
_____
_____
_____
_____

Peanut Butter Pancake Prerun Breakfast

Vincent and Emily Devlin run 100-mile marathons for enjoyment and personal challenge. They start their day with a 10-mile run around Mummy Mountain, in Paradise Valley. Devlin's pancakes gear them up.

　1/2 cup unbleached
　　or whole wheat flour
　2/3 cup nonfat dry milk powder
　1/3 cup wheat germ
　1/4 cup cornmeal
　2 teaspoons baking powder
　3 eggs, beaten
　2 tablespoons honey
　1/2 teaspoon vanilla
　3/4 cup creamy peanut butter
　1 cup water
　Buttermilk

Mix flour, milk powder, wheat germ, cornmeal, and baking powder. In separate bowl, beat eggs, add honey, vanilla, peanut butter, and water. Mix well. Add liquid ingredients to flour mixture. When creamy, add buttermilk until batter is right consistency for baking cakes outdoors on hot, oiled griddle, over the grill. Makes 12.

Sourdough Hot Cakes for 50

Irene Lindley is a no-foolin' cook who belongs to a group well aware of the fact that they live in what once was a war zone — site of Arizona's Tewksbury-Graham Feud. What ended it? Why, the homemakers' food. The *Pleasant Valley Homemakers Cookbook* is dedicated to those cooks. This recipe is a satisfactory way to make peace with everybody. It's hard to fight on a full stomach, so the Homemakers just kept on having big pancake breakfasts.

The night before, make your starter by dissolving 5 packages of dry yeast in 1 1/2 cups warm water. Add:

4 quarts milk
1/2 cup sugar
20 cups flour

Mix in glass or pottery (not metal) container and let stand at room temperature overnight. At serving time, add:

2 cups melted butter or
    cooking oil
20 eggs
3 tablespoons salt
3 teaspoons soda in
1/4 cup water

Mix well and bake hot cakes. Serves 50.

Pancakes go everywhere, and are welcome wherever they're cooked — picnic, patio, or campsite. Extras — even such surprises as peanut butter or chocolate — lend a touch of the unexpected; and sourdoughs are always special.

Whiskey Pancakes

Favorite foods and trail-ride shenanigans of the Cowboy Artists of America were tracked and noted by Tom Watson, their secretary-treasurer, business manager, honorary member, historian, and sometime trail-ride cook. In 1971, the CAA rode on the IX Ranch north of Big Sandy, Montana. Watson said he'd cook if artist Joe Beeler would man the fire.

"I'd heard of beer pancakes, so for one breakfast I decided to make whiskey pancakes," Watson wrote. "I mixed them up with Jack Daniel's. The batter was beautiful and fluffy; it smelled great. When John Hampton wanted seconds, he held out his plate and said, 'Pour me another one.'"

Grandfather Nebeker's Pancakes

I first interviewed Merry Nebeker in her Prescott kitchen back when Bill was showing great promise as a sculptor. He was so much into art that it threatened to interfere seriously with his favorite activity, hunting. Ten years later, life is only better. Bill is a member of the Cowboy Artists of America and now takes his whole family hunting. Merry says he loves an immense breakfast topped off with what his grandfather called German Pancakes. She has substituted biscuit mix, but the iron skillet is a must, at home or on family outings.
Fire should be steady.

    2 cups Bisquick
    1 1/2 cups milk
    2 eggs
    1 tablespoon cinnamon
    1 tablespoon sugar
    Vegetable oil

Combine first 5 ingredients until smooth, with the consistency of a sauce. Heat a small iron skillet to high, then add vegetable oil, just enough to cover lightly. Pour batter to thinly cover, tilting and moving the pan so the batter is evenly spread over the entire bottom. When golden brown, turn over gently. Pancakes will be very thin. Serve with warm butter, corn syrup, or jam, or just sprinkle with sugar. No guarantee that a diet of these will produce a sculptor.

Chocolate Pancakes

Patio breakfast or camping with the small fry on a cold day, it is up to the cook to top the menu with something new and exciting. Quick, easy, and good, even without syrup, are these pancakes made with only three ingredients. Make them thinner by adding more chocolate milk.

    2 cups Bisquick or your own
      biscuit mix
    1 2/3 cups chocolate milk
    1 egg

Combine in bowl and beat smooth with a beater if at home. At camp, shake or beat with fork in pouring vessel. Grease griddle if necessary. Turn when bubbles appear. Makes 12-14 small pancakes. Eat at once.

They can have even more special taste with cinnamon, cinnamon-sugar, or — don't freak out! — peanut butter. Let the children swoosh the centers with whipped cream. Roll 'em up for casual crepes; adults may add a spot of rum or Kahlúa to their cream.

Cowbelle Pan Cakes

Ranch wives cook on a budget that goes up and down with the price of beef. Mrs. James S. Allyn, clever wife of a Queen Creek cattlegrower and mother of three, whipped up economy beef dishes with flair. This is a Cowbelle's corn bread substitute for pizza — hearty and easy enough for breakfast any hour of the day, whomped together on the grill.

1 1/2 cups corn muffin mix
3/4 cup milk
1 egg
1 large garlic clove, minced
1 medium onion, chopped
2 tablespoons oil
1/2 pound ground chuck
3/4 teaspoon oregano
3/4 teaspoon chili powder
1-pound can tomatoes
2 tablespoons seasoned salt
1/3 cup tomato paste
1/2 green pepper, chopped
1 1/2 cups water

Combine corn muffin mix, milk, and egg, stirring until fairly smooth. In iron skillet, sauté garlic and onion in oil. When clear, add chuck and sauté until it loses red color. Stir in seasonings, liquid from canned tomatoes, tomato paste, green pepper, and water. Cover and simmer 15 minutes to cook flavors through. Meanwhile, in small buttered skillet, use 1/2 cup corn muffin batter for each of 4 thick pancakes. Keep warm. Add finely squashed tomatoes to meat sauce and bring to boil. On serving dish, stack pancakes alternately with meat sauce, generously sprinkling Parmesan or grated cheese between layers and on top. Serve in wedges to four.

Pancake Dividends

Once I was fortunate enough to be seated across the table from Charles Schultz, creator of the comic strip "Peanuts." In his soft-spoken, humorous way, he was discussing his family's traditional outdoor Saturday morning pancake breakfasts. His wife had discovered that adding melted butter and real maple syrup to the batter resulted in a whole new product. She said a dude ranch cook told her it was his secret. I like to think it was an Arizona dude ranch cook. It works — and it is just as delectable in waffle batter.

Funnel cakes are a way of life in Pennsylvania's Amish homes, and often a feature at fairs. It took Sheila Shelor, mom to five Phoenix pancake fans, to teach me that anyone with a funnel can spiral batter into hot oil — making golden-crisp names, numbers, or letters. If batter is too thick, add milk. If too thin, add flour. Covering bottom of funnel with finger, pour 1/3 cup batter into top. Remove finger and release batter into hot oil in 8-inch iron skillet. Drain on paper towels and serve with syrup or cinnamon-powdered sugar. A patio-perfect project. Fun diversion on a chilly camping day.

Crisp and appetizing, Mexican-French Toast is so rich that no butter is needed, and one slice may make a breakfast.

Camp Coffee to Suit 'em All

The late Roscoe Willson, Arizona historian, liked to recall a dude wrangler named Hades Church. Willson was along when Hades was packing six vacationing Californians into the Colorado River, with a mountain of gear and six hampers of food and dry ice.

When finally in camp, Hades announced he'd make the best coffee on either rim of the Grand Canyon. As he dipped handfuls of coffee into the pot, he gave his recipe:

"I put in a big handful for the fellow who likes it strong, and a little handful for the fellow who likes it weak. Then it suits everybody!"

Poolside Mexican-French Toast

Jane Mau came to Arizona and immediately lost the "cooped-up" feeling she had when weather-bound in New York. "The first summer, I only got out of the swimming pool to eat," she admitted. "Then I learned to cook or serve most of our meals by the pool. The family loves Mexican-French toast. It's higher, crisper, prettier, and remains hot and delectable longer than the average French-French toast."

2 cups flour
3 egg yolks, lightly beaten
1 cup sugar
1 teaspoon salt
1 1/2 (approx.) cups milk
3 beaten egg whites
8 slices firm, homestyle bread

Measure flour and fluff with fork. Beat egg yolks until foamy in bowl. Add sugar and salt and stir with enthusiasm. Blend in flour. Add milk to bring batter to consistency of pancakes. Fold in beaten egg whites. Dip bread in batter and coat well. Fry in peanut or sunflower oil heated to 360 degrees in electric fry pan. It is possible to fry 2 slices at once. Batter will puff and bubble and turn golden brown, covering each side of bread with a light, crusty covering, much like a Mexican sopapilla. When both sides are browned, remove and drain well on paper towels. Keep warm and serve quickly with jam or berry syrup and crisp bacon. These are so rich no butter is needed. One slice per person often suffices. Mexican-French Toast is a welcome nighttime snack, too.

Grilled Ham
& New Potatoes

My mother's family roots go back to the Pennsylvania hills. They ran the typical self-sufficient farm. As a child fortified with homemade bread, sweet butter, and pink smoked ham, I collected eggs. This grilled breakfast for camp or patio has a smoky robustness almost as good as that which emerged from my grandmother's big iron skillets. Grill or skillet, add apple chunks braised in maple syrup, crusty bread, and fresh eggs, and you can join me in nourishing nostalgia.

    2 slices well-cured ham, fat trimmed
    1/2 cup each, orange juice, brown sugar,
        and honey
    1/2 teaspoon dry mustard
    1 dozen little new potatoes
    3 tablespoons real butter
    Salt and pepper to taste
    1 tablespoon fresh, chopped parsley

Snip edges of ham so it won't buckle and curl. Place on grill over hot, gray coals. Stir together the orange juice, brown sugar, honey, and mustard. Baste ham slices constantly, turning once.

The new potatoes must be well-scrubbed and halved or quartered, with skins on. Arrange on generous length of heavy duty aluminum foil. Spread with butter, salt, pepper, and parsley. Use double-fold seal. Place on rack over hot, gray coals and grill 20 minutes. No onion, hear? Taste the potato. Apples can be cooked in another foil pack. Serves four. Old-fashioned pleasure on the patio or in camp.

Green Chile
Escalloped Potatoes

Shirley and Charles Cartwright grew up across the street from each other and married young, settling into the Cartwright School District, named after a pioneer branch of the family tree. As their family grew, she originated this escalloped potato brunch dish because Charles would eat almost anything with green chiles.

    6 large potatoes, peeled and sliced
    1 teaspoon salt
    1/2 teaspoon garlic salt
    Dash of pepper
    2 10-ounce cans cheddar cheese soup
    1 cup milk
    2 tablespoons flour
    1 4-ounce can diced green chiles, drained
    1/2 cup or more grated Longhorn cheese

Sprinkle seasonings and flour over potatoes placed in buttered 9 by 13-inch pan. Add cheese soup, chiles, and enough milk to cover potatoes. Bake 1 1/2 hours at 375 degrees, adding grated cheese the last 20 minutes. Serves eight. Wrapped in foil, then paper, this stays hot for hours.

Gary's Game Meat Italian Sausage

Gary Schneider, engineering executive, has hunted in every state but Alaska. When he and wife Jeannie settled in Scottsdale, they got serious about what Gary calls "domestic cooking" — special family recipes. One annual weekend project is making sausage.

> 10 pounds deer and/or
>   elk trimmings
> 10 pounds pork butt
> 2 tablespoons coarsely
>   ground black pepper
> 1 ounce fennel seeds
> Salt, garlic powder,
>   and hot pepper
>   flakes to taste

Coarsely grind both meats. Mix together by hand. Spread on flat surface. Pat to 1-inch thickness. Salt surface heavily. Sprinkle fennel seeds over all. Sprinkle black pepper, garlic, and pepper flakes over all. With hands, fold into mix. Mix heartily. Have a beer. Make a patty, fry it, and taste. Adjust the seasonings. Test again. Make into patties or put in casings, twisting every 5 inches. Freeze.

Instantly Breakfast

When Mary L. Cochran was president of the Arizona Federation of Garden Clubs, she spearheaded a carrot cookbook — every recipe containing carrots — to garner golden carats to fund a 50th-anniversary gift to the state. The clubs got their early-morning go-power from this mover-and-shaker breakfast.

> 1/2 banana, peeled
> 1 small carrot, scraped
> 1 egg
> 3/4 cup orange juice
> 1/3 cup nonfat dry milk
> 1 teaspoon honey, sugar,
>   or sweetener of choice, optional
> Cinnamon or nutmeg, if desired

Slice or dice banana and carrot. Put into blender with remaining ingredients, using sugar and spice, if wanted. Blend until thoroughly frothed. Mary says this drink even makes you see better! Ideal quickie after jogging, early tennis, or a morning hike.

Enchantment Granola

This is a showstopper in a book all camp and trail hearties should examine, *Gorp, Glop & Glue Stew*, by Prater and Mendenhall. There are as many recipes for granola as there are hikers. Most buy plain granola and add anything from raisins to banana flakes. Enchantment is for do-it-yourselfers.

> 5 cups rolled oats and whole-grain flakes
> 2 cups chopped raw almonds and walnuts
> 1 cup raw wheat, rice, or bran germ
> 1 cup natural, shelled sunflower seeds
> 1 cup safflower, sunflower, or canola oil
> 2 level teaspoons sea salt
> 1/2 cup pure maple syrup or honey

Preheat oven to 325 degrees. Mix ingredients in a big bowl, then spread into big roaster or pan, well-oiled. Bake 30 minutes or so, until toasty, stirring every 10 minutes. Stir again as Enchantment cools. If you find popular granola grows dull, add seeds, other nuts, dried fruits, or coconut. Yield: 9 to 10 cups. Seal in plastic bags and refrigerate. Eat any time.

Grits in a Ring

Hominy grits are the true grits of the South, but as the y'all people moved west, they found parched hominy in use rather than the more finely ground grits. Folks with Southern roots know grits make a satisfying and filling breakfast. In the West, however, hominy is more often a side dish or part of a boiled meal. Strange as it may seem to Southerners and Westerners alike, hominy baked with cheese and eggs is terrific with steak. Unfortunately, we now have instant grits, as deprived of nutrition as instant rice and instant oats. This recipe starts out boiling and ends up baking, using non-instant, so you can have a bowl for breakfast, then casserole the rest for use with grilled meat at dinner.

3/4 cup hominy grits
2 cups boiling water
1 teaspoon salt
1/2 pound sharp cheese
1 cup milk
2 eggs

Stir grits into salted boiling water in top of double boiler. Cover and cook over boiling water 45 minutes, stirring at times. When thickened, take out a serving for your breakfast. To the remaining, add cheese, milk, and eggs, and pour into buttered 8-inch ring mold. Bake 30 minutes at 350 degrees.

No-Cook Carbohydrate Breakfast

O*h, breakfast! Oh, breakfast!*
The meal of my heart.
Bring porridge, bring sausage, bring fish for a start.
Bring kidneys and mushrooms and partridge legs,
But let the foundation be bacon and eggs.
— A.P. Herbert, British breakfast booster

Time was when athletes ate almost-total-protein breakfasts, Herbert style. Then came the carbohydrate shift, and athletes as well as energetic outdoor types endorsed them as the best fuel source for energy, burning faster than fats. Alvan Adams, now retired from the Phoenix Suns of the National Basketball Association, fueled himself in his playing days with Birchermuesli, an ideal no-cook breakfast for camp or patio.

3 cups oatmeal, not instant
2 1/2 cups milk
3 tablespoons honey
1 teaspoon vanilla
1/2 cup raisins
Fresh fruit

Mix oatmeal, milk, honey, vanilla, and raisins. Refrigerate overnight. For a further energy breakfast, add fruit in season from apples to berries to bananas. "A Swiss doctor created this for his patients. It's great," Adams promised.

Pre-breakfast Jolts

Over the years, breakfast and brunch hosts often gave me freshly squeezed orange or tangerine juice as an eye-opener. (Almost as often, though, my host stirred a brisker eye-opener, a slightly modified Bloody Mary, adding the option of Tabasco and vodka with V-8 Juice.) My favorite hostess heated the same ingredients and added chicken broth, calling it a Cup o' Kindness.

Eye-Opener One. Shake or stir together: 1 16-ounce can V-8 Juice, 2 teaspoons fresh lemon or lime juice, 2 teaspoons Worcestershire Sauce, and a dash of salt — all pleasantly chilled. Offer Tabasco and/or vodka, to be stirred in with a celery stalk. Yield: 4 to 6 servings. Yes, some intrepid souls drop in an egg.

Cup o' Kindness. Heat the V-8 Juice, citrus juice, and Worcestershire Sauce with 2 chicken bouillon cubes, 1 cup water, a wisp of oregano, and a chop of fresh parsley. Simmer a few slow-roll minutes. Serve hot, with a thin slice of lemon and, again, Tabasco to taste. The vodka never made it into this bracer. Same yield.

Outpost Coffee

Most summers our family spent a week at a cabin in the Lakeside area. We made a Mormon friend when we admired his golden-haired, rosy-cheeked children. "No caffeine in them," he said. "Nor in me." "What do you drink instead of tea or coffee?" we asked. "Mormon Tea, sometimes, and Outpost Coffee, if my mother fixes it. Ground wheat if my wife makes some; or Postum." Outpost Coffee was roasted and sweetened like Arbuckle's; otherwise, very different.

2 quarts wheat bran
1 pint cornmeal
3 eggs, beaten
1 cup sorghum molasses

Mix together the wheat bran and the cornmeal, then blend together with the well-beaten eggs and molasses. Spread on a pan and put to dry in the oven, on low heat, about 275. Stir often to get a toasted, regular browning. The secret of good coffee is in the toasting. To make enough for 2, bring 2 cups of water to a boil, then stir in 2 tablespoons Outpost mixture. Allow to cook until coffee is as strong as desired. Add a little canned milk or fresh cream, and drink healthy.

White Chili

If you like arguments, count on chili, said to rank third after religion and politics on the list of "you can't win" controversies. When my friend, Vi Rukkila, pulled out an iron pot of White Chili, the argument began between vegetarian chiliheads and (almost unheard of) chicken chiliheads. The recipe is a Dutch-oven delight.

>   1 tablespoon corn oil
>   1 onion, chopped
>   1 clove garlic, minced
>   1 teaspoon cumin
>   2 large whole chicken breasts,
>   skinned and cooked
>   1 15-ounce can garbanzo beans, drained
>   1 15-ounce can white beans, drained
>   1 12-ounce can white corn, drained
>   2 4-ounce cans chopped green chiles
>   2 chicken bouillon cubes
>   1 1/2 cups boiling water
>   1 cup shredded Monterey Jack cheese

In Dutch oven, medium hot, cook onion, garlic, and cumin in hot oil. Mince or chop chicken breasts and, when onion and garlic are tender, stir in chicken, then add beans, corn, and chiles. Stir to blend. Combine chicken bouillon with 1 1/2 cups boiling water, and stir through chili. Cover and let chili cook over low coals or heat, or in ashes, until flavors blend — about 30 minutes. Stir with wooden spoon, as both beans and corn have tendency to scorch or stick if heat is too high. Just before serving, sprinkle cheese over top. Return cover for a few minutes. Serve with red or green salsa or sauce, but there goes the White Chili. Serves six with tortillas and salad. This also can be made in a large electric cooker and toted to picnics and ball games.

(OPPOSITE PAGE) *Chicken in chili? Try White Chili before leaping to negative conclusions. It's a Dutch oven delight, served with tortillas and a salad.*

Outdoor Food for Bird Watchers

Most bird watchers care little for cooking on the trail. They are sandwich people — or snackers — as birds are, and some are cookie crumblers. Many carry a thermos of hot tea, not coffee. One of my favorite Arizona bird watchers is Catherine Noble. She led a group to Mexico. She loved birds, but her surprise, arranged ahead of time with a creative Mexican cook, was a feast of 2 dozen wild ducks, dressed in a sauce so ripe with rum that nobody could remember next morning what else they had eaten. It's one of my favorite memories; rarely have I seen a more congenial crowd.

My editor says he could never take a sandwich on a hike. He did once, a thick, healthy one. "It was a killer," he says. "You can't digest a big sandwich and hike."

Bird watchers are not out for the hike. They are out to look and to be quiet and to deal in stealth. Like Catherine, they'll save up for dinner.

Favorite choices are hunks of pumpernickel or Logan bread, a square of cheddar or Gouda cheese (both well wrapped in whatever you plan to carry back home), and a fresh pear or apple. Plant the cores well. Or take journey cakes that you've baked (see Bean Ball, Chapter 12), or most fitting, Seed Cakes from the Sierra Club's terrific publication, *Simple Foods for the Pack*.

CHAPTER 5

Vegetating

Not long ago there were three basic vegetables ordained to be served with barbecued meals: beans, potatoes, and corn. Beans, either in the Dutch oven or canned, usually came with bacon and brown sugar, or chiles and garlic. They were number one. Potatoes, baked brown and bursting from their skins, vied with corn on the cob, inviting yellow kernels adrip with real butter, for second place at the plate. That was it: beans, potatoes, corn.

Overnight, "nouvelle grill" opened the garden gate, and any vegetable known to the produce department is fair game. Do not expect these to look beautiful.

Brown, yes. Grill-treaded, yes. Tasty. Smoky. Easy. Yes to all. And, if you leave the grill unattended, also charred. A minor outdoor cooking adventure is possible for anyone ready to slice an eggplant or wrap goat cheese in cooked cabbage leaves.

No matter the site — trail, camper, patio, or waterside — my advice is a proven Arizona truth. Always have on hand a package of good flour tortillas and a gurgle of hot sauce. A drift of grated cheese helps, too. Wrapped in this trio, the most fire-dried or half-raw vegetable takes on new life. Eat fast.

(OPPOSITE PAGE) *Almost too beautiful to eat, but too delicious to ignore, a pansy salad is decorated by a variety of greens, including arugula, spinach, and radicchio.*

Vegetable Kabobs with Patio Sauce

"Life happens at a different pace here; the climate is inducive to more time to enjoy the good things of life . . . including the art of cooking . . ."

Barbara Kraus wrote that about Tucson in the cookbook, *Purple Sage and Other Pleasures*. Make this up where you will; sauce, grill, and savor it on the patio.

Patio Sauce
1 8-ounce can tomato sauce
2 tablespoons molasses
1 tablespoon cider vinegar
1/4 teaspoon dried tarragon leaves
1/8 teaspoon dried mustard

Combine in a small bowl and mix well. Brush generously on vegetables which have been threaded on 8-inch skewers. Broil or grill 3 minutes on each side.

Suggested vegetables: Blanched zucchini and eggplant, sliced and cubed; bell peppers in sixths; small, whole parboiled onions; cherry tomatoes; large mushrooms; corn on the cob in 2-inch pieces.

(LEFT) *Grill time usually conjures up visions of meat, fowl, or seafood over the open fire, but don't forget the wonderful way outdoor cooking enhances the flavors of fresh vegetables. With a hand-held basket, the cook easily controls temperature by moving veggies toward or away from the coals.*

Speed Grilling

Totem Pole Potatoes: While a charcoal fire is burning down to the necessary gray ash, put 2 or 3 tall juice cans on the grill, holding well-scrubbed, small, round potatoes on skewers. Fill cans with boiling, lightly salted water and let the potatoes cook until tender. Remove from cans with care and a heavy glove. Brush with butter, oil, or margarine and sprinkle with salt, pepper, chili powder, herbs, or paprika. Then, a few minutes over the coals will produce that grill glaze.

Popper French Fries. A quick answer to the potato problem. Thaw frozen fries on a cookie sheet in 1 layer. Then, a handful or more at a time, brown in a corn popper over the coals. Let the hungriest guest shake the popper.

Gallons of Garbanzos Salad

Five-bean salad for the annual picnic of the Northern Arizona Pioneers Historical Society, Inc., was tossed by the gallon in her Sky Ranch kitchen by Mrs. Homer L. Bullion. It became almost as popular as the playback of past events.

1 gallon garbanzo beans
1 gallon red kidney beans
1 gallon green lima beans
1 gallon cut green beans
1 gallon yellow wax beans
1 gallon cider vinegar
5 pounds sugar
1 pint sweet pickle relish
1 large bottle stuffed olives
6 green bell peppers, chopped
1 bunch celery, diced
1 pint cooking oil
4 small cans pimentos
1 small can celery seed
Sweet basil
Chopped chives

Drain juice from all cans to save for soup stock. Heat vinegar and sugar, stirring to dissolve. Cool with a little ice. Mix all ingredients in 8- or 10-gallon ranch kettle. Let it stand at least 2 hours, but flavor is best if beans are cooled and kept overnight. Serves 100. For just a few pioneers, reduce can size to quarts and use only 3 cups each of vinegar and sugar, cutting amounts of vegetables and herbs to taste.

Molly's Chileajo Vegetables

Molly Beverly is Arizona's garlic gastronome. When she is not growing, pulling, trimming, packing, and braiding garlic in Chino Valley, she is in her farm kitchen. This Mexican marriage of garlic and chiles is vegetarian as given. Add 1 or more cups of precooked chicken or pork (grilled is most flavorful) for even more strength.

4 medium, dried hot chiles, stemmed, seeded, deveined
6 large cloves garlic, unpeeled
1 cup green beans, 1/2-inch chopped
2/3 cup peas, fresh or frozen
2 small red boiling potatoes, skinned and diced
2 small carrots, peeled and diced fine
1 large pinch of ground cloves
1/4 teaspoon ground pepper
1/2 teaspoon oregano (or I use cumin)
1 tablespoon vegetable oil
1/2 teaspoon each, salt and sugar
1 1/2 tablespoons cider vinegar
12 corn tortillas
1/2 cup crumbled Mexican cheese
1/2 small onion, finely chopped

Soak chiles in boiling water 30 minutes. Drain. Roast unpeeled garlic cloves on a hot, dry skillet, turning often until blackened in spots and soft. Cool, then slip off skins. Place garlic and chiles in blender jar with 1/2 cup water. Add cloves, black pepper, and oregano (or cumin), and blend until smooth.

Bring several quarts of salted water to a boil in a large kettle. One at a time, boil until just tender: green beans, 3-5 minutes; fresh peas, 4-10 minutes; potatoes, 5 minutes; carrots, 5-8 minutes. Frozen peas, no cooking. As soon as each batch is done, run under cold water to stop cooking. Drain on paper towels. Transfer to mixing bowl with defrosted peas.

Heat oil in iron skillet at medium, adding chile sauce and stirring constantly until darker and thicker, 3 minutes. Reduce heat to medium low. Stir in vinegar. Thin chile paste with water to make a sauce. Simmer and add salt and sugar. Mix sauce into vegetables (and meat, if desired) and cover to blend flavors.

To serve, heat tortillas on grill (in foil) or in iron skillet. Pile 2 heaping tablespoons vegetables on each tortilla and top with cheese and onion. Serves six; two each. After, chew parsley or mint.

Hopi Pit-baked Corn

To look at this steaming brown corn with its rich, nutty aroma, it is hard to believe it was roasted months ago, then dried and, at cooking time, reconstituted. Marlinda Graham of Phoenix goes back to the Hopi reservation for corn each fall. Harvesting is something to look forward to in her estimation. The young people join the old men to pull the ripe corn from the stalks. The baking pit has been dug 7 or more feet deep and about 6 feet across. Dry wood is burned in it all day, as Marlinda tells it:

"We keep the fire going from 5 a.m. to about 1, or until it comes to a fine, soft ash. Then they put the green corn in and close it up. The men tromp the corn down tight and husks are put over the top. Then clean sand. It cooks by steam and smells so good. It is done in a few hours and we all help unpack it and eat some right then. In fact, the first one we peel is the one we eat. We all help peel the corn and pile it up. If it is brown, it has been cooked right. It should not be too light. We string the corn up with yucca fiber to dry in the sun and when we take them down they are stored in a barrel.

"Whenever we want some, we put it in water and cook it. Plain water. I don't think anyone ever tried it with salt or sugar or anything else but water. The kernels become real tender again, and sweet. It is ready to eat, good as new."

(BELOW) The versatile ear of corn can be wrapped in foil for roasting, nestled into the coals in its own husks, baked in a pit, Hopi-style, or prepared this way — in the equally versatile Dutch oven.

Corn on the Cob

Indian-style roasting ears are for those who like brown, sweeter corn. Turn back the husks and strip off the silk. Wet the husks, re-covering the kernels. Line ears up on the grill over low coals and keep turning them often for about 20 minutes, depending on the heat. Remove when they are lightly bronzed. The longer corn roasts, the chewier and sweeter it gets. Serve with salt and butter and twist off the husks as they cool.

Foiled corn is juicier. Remove husks and butter corn, then wrap in foil and roast over coals 20-30 minutes. Some cooks wrap each ear in a strip of thin, lean bacon before double-wrapping in foil.

A common picnic way to roast corn is to soak the ears at least 30 minutes in cold water before stripping the husks back and removing the silks. When clean of silk, wrap husks in place over corn, tie with string or a strip of corn husk at the end of each ear, and foil wrap. Roasting then results in a steamed, juicy treat, needing only butter and salt for satisfaction.

Trail Mix Bean Salad

After two heart bypass surgeries, Joy Smith settled into exercise concentrated in one area, her two-mile daily walk on a Scottsdale canal bank. "Living is more important than eating," she discovered. She keeps this high-fiber salad mixed and ready to eat at any time. For hikes, mix beans in one heavy plastic bag; dressing in a little container. Toss as needed.

> 1/3 cup safflower oil
> 2/3 cup vinegar
> 1/2 cup sugar
> 1 cup finely diced onion and green pepper
> 1 16-ounce can garbanzo beans
> 1 16-ounce can red kidney beans
> 1 16-ounce can green or wax beans

Shake together oil, vinegar, sugar, onion, and green pepper. Toss over mixture of drained beans. Refrigerate. Double for a crowd. Perfect with barbecue.

Kelling Red Onion Salad

Kathie Kelling teaches positive body image classes which combine exercise, body awareness, relaxation, and visualization. All include a positive attitude about good food. Relaxation comes in the fresh air with this red onion cruncher. Visualize and prepare it early in the morning.

> 1 sweet red onion, in rings
> 1 can Mandarin oranges, drained, or
> 1 cup fresh seedless tangerine slices
> 1 cup Spanish peanuts
> 4 cups mixed salad greens
> **Toss with Ruth's Dressing**

Ruth's Dressing. 1 cup olive or peanut oil, 1/3 cup cider or wine vinegar, 1/3 cup sugar, 1 teaspoon dry mustard, 2 tablespoons celery seed, 1 small chopped onion, and salt and pepper to taste. Pour chilled dressing over all to serve to four hungries.

(BELOW) Corn relish can be another welcome "take-along" when the major part of the cooking is to be done outdoors — in camp, on a picnic, or just on the patio. Ingredients may include red peppers and tomatoes for a colorful contrast to the yellow corn — plus whatever the creative cook commands.

(LEFT)*The picnic or patio dip may be tame or wild, but hungry dippers usually enjoy this way of getting their fresh vegetables — radishes, carrots, broccoli, cauliflower, and more.*

Big Tiny Little's Broccoli Crunch

After 38 years on the road, the oceans, and assorted foreign countries, Big Tiny Little settled his piano in Arizona. He and his Nancy knew this was the place for the many outdoor recipes they piled up in years of motor home and cruise boat living.

1 cup broccoli flowerettes
1 cup fresh or frozen green peas
1 cup cauliflower chunks
1/2 cup sour cream or Imo
2 tablespoons mayonnaise
Garlic, optional

Lightly mix all ingredients, crunchy-best when served cold. Frozen peas thaw just enough to hold the chill. If taking a fishing or picnic jaunt, bag vegetables at home and mix dressing to add on the spot. Serves three or four.

Notes

_____
_____
_____
_____
_____
_____
_____
_____
_____
_____

Billie Jo's Poolside Salad

"Celebrate your body," is Billie Jo Donavon's message to the world. An exercise consultant, lithe Billie Jo has survived cancer surgery twice. "I drastically changed my diet, and I learned that water exercise can be a complete physical fitness program," she says. She advises, "Entertain, exercise, and visit in the pool. Then crawl out and serve lunch on the deck."

1 to 3 large heads butter lettuce
1 can Mandarin oranges, chilled
1 avocado, skinned and diced
1/2 cup fresh mushrooms
1/2 cup sliced or whole almonds

Have butter lettuce ready, washed, dried, and torn in bite-size pieces. Fill large salad bowl and top with drained oranges. Alternate avocado and mushroom slices with oranges. Drizzle on Poppy Seed Dressing and scatter with almonds.
Poppy Seed Dressing. 2/3 cup cider vinegar, 1 teaspoon dry mustard, 1 cup sugar, 3 tablespoons onion juice, 2 cups vegetable oil, 1 teaspoon salt, and 3 tablespoons poppy seeds.

Chapter 6

Fruitables

Apples, pears, cherries, berries, and other fruitables take on exciting new flavor when cooked with care over coals. Fruits rarely demand much heat. Usually they can be cooked, packaged in foil, at the sidelines of the grill or fire while the main dish is playing center court. You can broil fruits on the grill or under cover. You can protect them with heavy-duty foil, then set them on the coals or, in some cases, in the ashes.

Fruit is the ideal light, sweet, healthy, fairly quick ending to a meal. Sauces, fruit liqueurs, and that old standby, rum, are used often to glamorize those desserts. So, flambé the bananas or pears. And of course dried fruits are the reliable trail buddies we all reach for when hiking and camping. Citrus, so well-packaged by Mother Nature, is a friend in any campsite situation.

Fruit does a happy balancing act on the grill with barbecue, which is usually spicy, often hot. When prepared ahead, most fruit desserts or side dishes take only 5 to 15 minutes over the coals. Caution: Hang in there most of that time. Crisp and charred do nothing for the delicate flavors of fruits. Kabob it, wrap it in bacon or ham, drizzle with spice or honey butters, splash it with champagne, soak it in its liqueur cousin, or pique it with lime juice, but do not burn it.

(OPPOSITE PAGE) *Whether broiled, raw, sauced, glazed, or plain, bite-size chunks of fresh fruit are an important part of the outdoor cooking agenda. Strawberries, kiwi, pineapple, and just about any variety of melon add color, tempting flavor, and nutrition.*

Pineapple Pleasure

Cut clean, fresh pineapples lengthwise into quarters or sixths, depending on size, leaves and all. (Wrap leaves in a twist of heavy-duty foil to protect them from the fire.) Brush fruit with melted butter and grill until rippled brown. A dash of ginger or cinnamon and a brush of honey can be used as a last-minute glaze. Buddies well with ribs, ham, or pork. In a hurry, canned slices are easy.

Love for Three Oranges

Grate a little zest from 3 each, navel oranges, blood oranges, and Kinnowor mandarin oranges. Slice off tops and bottoms. Cut, peel and all, in thick slices. Pop out any seeds. Dip in butter or sunflower oil. Broil quickly on both sides. Sprinkle with zest and a flirt of nutmeg, or splash lightly with Cointreau or other orange liqueur. Terrific with duck, game, or chicken. Serves six.

Chilled Peach Soup

Each May, Pam Rhoads and husband Richard Embery gather family and friends to pick peaches in the Queen Creek area. Some fruit goes directly into the annual "peach daiquiri fest," usually as soon as possible after the trek to the orchards. But Pam manages to freeze about 6 quarts of peaches each year. The year-round fruits of their labors include pies, cobblers, or thawed fruit, mixed with a little peach brandy, and spooned over ice cream.

Peach soup, a family favorite, adapts to any dining situation — poolside, picnic, with bread or muffins as a main course, or as a dessert, with pound cake and fresh blueberries or raspberries.

2 one-pound bags frozen peaches, or
10 medium-size fresh peaches,
   peeled and pitted
1 1/2 cups softened vanilla ice cream
1/2 cup half-and-half
1/4 cup white wine
1/4 teaspoon freshly ground nutmeg
1/2 cup sugar (approx.)

Puree the peaches in food processor or blender. Add ice cream, half-and-half, wine, and nutmeg; blend until smooth. Add sugar to taste, and chill at least 2 hours before serving.

Peralta Apples

Phoenix cherishes ownership of the largest municipal no-fee park in the nation on sprawling South Mountain. The park staff teaches innovative outdoor cooking — bright, easy meals for small fees. Peralta Apples (Pedro Peralta was said to be the original finder of the fabled Lost Dutchman Gold Mine in the Superstition Mountains) are a genuine bonanza with camp pancakes

3 large apples, cored and sliced
2 tablespoons butter or bacon drippings
1/3 cup firmly packed brown sugar
Dash of salt
1 teaspoon cinnamon
1/3 cup raisins
1/3 cup chopped pecans or walnuts

Sauté apple slices in butter or bacon drippings until slices become limp. Add remaining ingredients and stir lightly. Cook briefly until apples are evenly coated with cinnamon sugar. Sensational over pancakes or French toast. Serves six, with bacon (optional), and coffee, cocoa, or hot tea.

Backpackers may prefer to use 1 1/2 cups dried apples soaked for 1 hour.

Apples on Strings or Sticks

Dried Apples. Know your apples and select only the tart, solid varieties for drying. Pippins, Gravensteins, Granny Smiths are what you need. If they're free of blemishes, check for the shipper's friend — wax. Wash those shiny beauties with castile soap, rinse, and dry well. Tunnel out the core. Slice apples no more than 1/4-inch thick. String a big, heavy-duty needle and run the string through the center of the sliced fruit. Allow space so slices do not touch. Hang in airy, dry or sunny room — even the attic if you're lucky enough to have one. Or use a fruit drier or clean screen covered with glass. Allow 2 or 3 days. Bag in plastic, ready to use in cereal or granola, or reconstituted into apple pies with crumb crusts.

Stick Apples. Again, wash and dry tart apples. Clean sticks. One apple per stick is the rule. Revolve over coals until skin shines and pops. Have ready a tin or plate with a mixture of sugar and cinnamon. Roll hot apples in sugar mix, then back to the fire until sugar melts and drips. Slice to eat, or just nibble off the stick.

Yes, We Have the Bananas

After living in the West Indies, Lori and Bart Pann moved to Phoenix. They re-created island life in their back patio. It took 5 years, with steady watering, before they had a small producing banana plantation. Lori's banana recipes became her stock in trade at their barbecues. They work just as successfully for store bananas.

Bananas in Blankets

6 large bananas, peeled
    and halved, crosswise
1/4 cup lemon juice, fresh
1/2 cup sugar, brown or granulated
12 slices very thin smoked ham or bacon

Preheat grill — kettle or covered type — to low, steady heat. Dip bananas in lemon juice. Sprinkle lightly with sugar. Wrap in ham or bacon slices and place in grill pan, meat edges underneath. Grill, covered, until glazed, about 12 to 15 minutes. You may want to crisp-broil the bacon 1 or 2 minutes. A conversation piece for brunch. Serves six.

Go Bananas on the Grill

6 large bananas, unpeeled
Light brown sugar
Sour cream, optional

Place bananas on edge of grill about 3 inches from heat. Grill, turning occasionally, until skins burst and juices bubble through. Using tongs, remove at once to foiled cookie sheet. Cool enough to peel. With spatula, arrange carefully on serving dish. Sprinkle with brown sugar and top with dollops of sour cream. Another option is to drizzle plain bananas with lime juice and honey.

Maple Syrup Banana Cake

6 firm bananas
2 tablespoons melted butter
1/2 cup maple syrup (real is best)
1/2 cup chopped nuts

Put peeled bananas into Pam-sprayed or oiled grill pan, or make a grill pan from doubled heavy foil, sides squared, about 2 inches high. Pour nuts and syrup over bananas which have been brushed with melted butter. Allow to heat and glaze at the edge of the grill over low heat, or bake in medium heat. Either way, 15-18 minutes should do it. The Panns think a very light sprinkle of salt before cooking keeps this from being too sweet. Another option is to serve as dessert with rum-whipped cream.

Fruit Leather

This golden oldie is made in as many variations as gorp, with but one unchanging ingredient — fruit.

Almost any fruit, although *The Sierra Club Pocket Food Book* suggests peaches, plums, all berries, apricots, and apple or pear sauce. Its recipe calls for putting clean, dry fruit through a ricer, whole, leaving just the dry peels or seeds in the ricer. Flavor may be expanded by honey, lemon juice, or almond extract. Pour into glass cake or pie pan and spread thin like apple butter. Dry in the sun by day; bring in at night to avoid dew. Repeat until dry, 3-4 days. When finished, the fruit looks like burnished leather. Peel off the pan and roll up in wax paper or plastic wrap. Store in cool, dry place in a plastic bag.

Other recipes suggest blending whole clean fruit in blender until almost liquid. Place in pan with sugar to taste and bring to a boil. Cool to warm. Spoon onto plastic wrap. Dry in sun several days or, in cold weather, dry under the heat of several lamps.

For variety, leather can be sprinkled while wet with granola, fine coconut, powdered sugar, or ground nuts or seeds. Roll and store when completely dry. Break off pieces of leather to melt in your mouth as you hike or fish. It's a healthier snack pickup than the hard-candy "sugar bombs" many use as an energy booster.

Pineapple-Banana Sherbet

1 tablespoon gelatin
1/4 cup cold water
1 cup crushed pineapple with juice
3/4 cup light honey
2 cups buttermilk
3 tablespoons fresh lemon juice
1/2 pint whipping cream, whipped
2 or 3 mashed ripe bananas
1 teaspoon vanilla

Soften gelatin in cold water; dissolve by stirring over hot water in double boiler. Stir pineapple and honey into gelatin. Remove from heat and mix well. In bowl, add to buttermilk and lemon juice. Fold in whipped cream, crushed banana, and vanilla. Freeze in ice cube trays or cake pans in freezer 2 or 3 hours, stirring once an hour. When smooth, spoon into waxed cups and refreeze for easy serving. Kids love 'm-m-m-m. Serves 10-12.

Painted Pears

Begin with big, ripe, but firm pears, but don't forget sweet little pears for contrast with their grilled aunts. Slice the little ones thin and sprinkle with apple juice so they won't discolor. Halve and core the big pears and brush with butter or peanut oil. Grill skin-side down 3 or 4 minutes. Turn and grill 4 more minutes, peeking to make sure the interesting grill lines have not turned black. To serve, take a choice. Fill cavities with cheddar or blue cheese and top with a perfect pecan half. Or shave dark or semisweet chocolate over pears while warm, but not hot. Fill cavities with a little cream cheese and a few ripe, green grapes.

Pears can take almost any grilled apple recipe. Hard pears can be cored, filled with a little butter or Gouda cheese and cinnamon, wrapped in heavy foil, and baked on the outer edge of the grill. Or fill an oven grill pan with overlapping slices of pear and roast them, grill cover down, 10 or 12 minutes. Glaze with honey and rum a few minutes. Serve with whipped cream.

Chillers

Sherbets, granitas, sorbets, juice-sicles, and frozen fruit yogurts are lapped up year around in Arizona with its 300-plus days a year of sunshine. Here are samples of fruit freezes perfect for backyard dining or after-swim stargazing on the patio.

Peachy Lime Granita

1 1/2 cups ripe peaches, pitted and chopped
1 1/2 teaspoons fresh lime juice
1/4 cup sugar
1 cup water

In a blender or food processor, puree the peaches and lime juice. Stir sugar and water in saucepan and simmer 5 minutes. Cool. Mix with peach blend and transfer to 2 metal ice trays without dividers. Freeze, stirring lumps to smooth every half hour, for 2 to 3 hours. Granita is meant to be more coarse-grained than sherbet (it's okay if you want to call it sherbert, Herbert), and is served as a palate cleanser or a light, cool-down dessert. It's especially nice after chile dishes or meats. Recipe makes a quart.

Fruit Sorbet

This type of sorbet is called "sugarless," but because they are made from very ripe fruits, all of which contain fruit sugars, I'll simply call them delectable. If you are moneyed enough to have a Champion juicer, they are a snap. Freeze melons, chunks of peeled and cut pineapple and banana, peel-on peaches, plums, and nectarines, and whole berries, stemmed. Put in any combination and out of the juicer comes smooth instant sorbet. You can get the same result with a food processor, but the fruit is liquid enough that it must be returned to the freezer.

Juice-sicles

Into small cups or ice cube trays with dividers, pour chilled, fresh, unsweetened fruit juice of choice. Freeze until mushy. Insert wooden sticks before juice is frozen solid. Extra taste appeal for children if you add finely grated carob, chocolate, coconut, or fruit.

Frozen Fruit Yogurt

For each cup of unsweetened yogurt, add 1 1/2 cups fresh berries, peaches, or apricots, using half a very ripe banana for sweetener — or honey or maple syrup to taste. Freeze for a light lunch or refreshing dessert.

For hikers' and kids' lunch boxes (or for dieters), this fruit-and-yogurt mix can be poured into thermoses — not too full — and put into the freezer without lids. Next day, seal and carry away for a refreshing, healthy lunch. This idea came from Whitaker and Flournoy's innovative *Nature's Kitchen*.

Smooth, instant sorbet from the juicer or food processor tops off any patio dinner or luncheon. In this case, it started with raspberries and pineapple.

Peg's Scalloped Pineapple

For a forget-calories picnic or patio meal, I use my sister-in-law Peggy's never-a-crumb-left casserole, especially good with grilled ham, sausages, or hot dogs. It's best eaten at a picnic table on the edge of the woods at sundown, just before the current year's crop of fawns ventures out to browse.

    4 cups raisin bread cubes
    1 No. 202 can crushed pineapple
        with juice
    1/2 cup butter
    1 cup sugar
    1 pinch salt
    3 eggs
    1/2 cup milk

Cream together butter and sugar. Add eggs and beat thoroughly. Add remaining ingredients. Pour into oiled or buttered 2-quart casserole. Bake 1 hour at 350 degrees. Wrap well in foil, then in newspaper to transport. Stays hot 2 hours. Serves eight.

Leftover Blessing

As the camping or trail trip winds down and food is reduced to bits, make the final fire meal special with a fruit crisp in foil. Soak leftover dried fruit in hot water with a little lemon juice. Chop that withered apple or pear, dice a date or fig.

Melt a little butter with brown sugar or honey and 1 cup of granola dregs, cereal powder from the bottom of the bag, and wisps of coconut or a few nutmeats or sunflower seeds. Top fruit with mixture and bake on top of grill in small fry pan or in a double layer of foil, folded over and sealed. Give it 12 to 15 minutes over camp stove or coals. Usually you wind up with enough to share.

N o t e s

Chapter 7

Sauces, Marinades, & Zappers

When we consider sauces, homage to the French first comes to mind — unless we're Southwest natives. Here, food is stung to life by that simmering Mexican standby, Red Chile Sauce, and its uncooked cousin, *Salsa Cruda*. Japanese-Americans add zip with the gentle *shoyu*, or soy sauce, and the freshness of fish sauce. Americans of Chinese origin know the subtle luxury of oyster sauce. And, of course, Italians have made food history with pesto and tomato sauces.

To further gild the cooking lily, Grandmother's Chile Sauce and Mom's White Sauce share space with other sauces such as mustard, mushroom, curry, steak, and a flotilla of barbecue sauces. Glazes and butter-rum serve the sweet tooth.

Sauces, then, elevate food flavor. Marinades invade the soul of sole and flank, tenderizing as they penetrate. Zappers, like zesty, dry-mop toppers, contribute the "mouth of hell" delight sought by many outdoor cooks.

Do we find all these sauces-plus in outdoor cooking? Aye, and more. On patios, at picnics, on the gourmet trail with upscale campers, sauces and marinades are here to stay.

(OPPOSITE PAGE) *When the saga of southwestern sauces is written, Mexican-style salsa will provide the leading chapter. The ingredients are many and varied (just look at the samples around the bowl), but flavorful, zesty chiles are always there in full force.*

Spartan "Secret" Barbecue Sauce

Orval Braunbeck hosted a pig picking for every welder and electrician, contractor and supplier who had helped bring a major building project to completion ahead of schedule. It was the best barbecue I ever tasted, and he even gave me the recipe. On chops or loins, a gallon will do four home-grill pig pickin's.

2 sticks (1/2 pound) butter
1 large bottle (20-ounce)
    Kraft Barbecue Sauce
Crushed red peppers
Worcestershire Sauce
1 gallon apple cider vinegar

Heat the butter and Kraft's sauce. Mix with peppers and Worcestershire to your own taste. Stir in vinegar. Start moppin' on pork chops, roast, quarters, or the whole pig, over low, steady coals. Serve with beans, potato salad, corn bread, chilled soft drinks, and beer.

Tart, No-catsup Barbecue Sauce

Most barbecue sauce recipes lead off with catsup. Then (hurrah!) came Sharon Barger, a Phoenix therapist who paints in oils, plays the baritone uke and guitar, and entertains by barbecuing. Chicken, pork, and ribs are anointed, both sides, with this tart, peppery, no-catsup sauce.

1 quart vinegar
2 garlic cloves, minced
2 medium onions, chopped
2 tablespoons prepared mustard
2 teaspoons each, salt and black pepper
Juice of 1 lemon
2 tablespoons sugar
2 tablespoons Worcestershire Sauce
2 tablespoons A-1 Sauce
1 tablespoon red pepper
1/4 pound butter

Simmer 30 minutes. Makes 1 1/2 quarts. Keep indefinitely, refrigerated. Good therapy for any grilled meat.

Italian Barbecue Baste

Putsee Vannucci came to Benson from Williamsport, Pennsylvania, to experience the small-town West. He added an oregano touch to western barbecue and surprised everyone with his baste brush. "To be authentically Italian, apply the sauce to the meat with a brush of fresh mint leaves," he advises.

2 tablespoons peanut or olive oil
2 cups canned, peeled tomatoes,
    well-mashed
2 small garlic cloves,
    finely chopped
1 teaspoon oregano
1 teaspoon freshly
    snipped parsley
1/4 cup olive oil
Salt and pepper to taste
Fresh mint leaves

Brown fowl or meat lightly in peanut or olive oil, on both sides. Combine remaining ingredients and blend well. If mint leaves are not available, use barbecue brush or mop. Arrange fowl or meat on grill, over gray-hot coals. Brush on sauce. Grill 5-10 minutes. Turn and brush other side. Continue to turn and brush faithfully until done to taste. This baste not only adds a great, unsweet flavor, but it helps retain juices. Enough for one or two chickens or two to three steaks. Use any remaining baste as a sauce for dipping as you eat. And happy *ciao*-ing.

Dottie's AZ-Tex Barbecue Best

From the first time Dottie Embery stirred and simmered this chili-lemon-cumin-plus barbecue sauce for her family of 8, it was declared perfect. When Dottie's son Richard came to Arizona, this recipe came, too. In years of photographing spectacular food in a spectacular way (check this book), he never found a better sauce.

1 cup chopped onion
1 clove garlic, chopped
1/4 cup vegetable oil
2 tablespoons chili powder
2 cups catsup
1 cup vinegar
1/2 cup fresh lemon juice
1/4 cup Worcestershire Sauce
1/3 cup brown sugar
2 tablespoons dry mustard
1 tablespoon salt
2 teaspoons dry cumin
2 tablespoons butter

Slowly sauté onion in oil until tender, about 10 minutes, adding garlic at the end of the cooking period. Stir in chili powder and cook 1 minute. Add everything but butter. Bring to a boil, then reduce to a simmer for 30 minutes. Stir butter in last. Yield: 5-6 cups.
It's a hurrah!

Gwen's Las Madrinas Marinade

Many men shy at inside kitchen duty, yet become paragons at the outside fire. Gwen and Keith Nemmers moved to Scottsdale and were lured quickly to outdoor cooking. This marvelous marinade transforms chicken. Even better, it transformed Keith into a chef — outside only.

1/4 cup melted butter or margarine
2 tablespoons sugar
1/4 teaspoon Tabasco Sauce
1/2 teaspoon dry mustard
1/3 cup salad oil
1/4 cup catsup
2 tablespoons cider vinegar
1 tablespoon Worcestershire Sauce
1 small onion, chopped fine

Combine to make 1 1/2 cups. Marinate chicken pieces (1 to 2 chickens) 1/2 hour as coals burn down. Transfer chicken to grill and keep turning and basting until golden-done, about 1/2 hour.

Basic Chile Sauce

You need a recipe for good chile sauce because it's a basic for other sauces as well as a sidewinder for meats. I inherited this recipe, but what a surprise to get the same recipe from Mildred Cropp of the Phoenix Baptist Hospital Auxiliary. She had neatly condensed the directions, though, to two sentences.

1 gallon washed, cut tomatoes, red
3 large onions, skinned and chopped
1 pint vinegar
1 pint sugar
1 hot pepper, chopped
1 tablespoon salt
1 teaspoon celery salt, rounded

Combine and put on stove; cook slowly 1 or 2 hours or until thick; stir every little bit. When thick, put in hot, sterilized jars and seal. I should add: Choose the hot pepper according to your own taste, deseeding and deveining for the tender palate.

Sauce the Onions

Chives commonly green up the tops of baked potatoes. If the market or garden has been chived-out, green onions in a butter and milk sauce offer a three-in-one alternative. Just slice up a cup of fresh onions with tops to cook in 1/4 cup of butter until soft. Remove from grill and blend in 2 tablespoons flour with salt and freshly ground white pepper to taste. Slowly add a cup of milk and return to heat, stirring until creamy. When potatoes come out of the coals, split tops, pour sauce over, and accept compliments graciously. Makes a generous cup-and-a-half of sauce, enough for 6 to 8 potatoes.

Easy to bake in the coals or on the grill (especially if nudged along by ahead-of-time microwaving, then finished on the open fire), potatoes can be heaven in a brown jacket. Onions, chives, bacon bits, grated cheese — or the onion sauce described above — are among the enhancers.

Grand Canyon White Sauce

You don't have to be Colin Fletcher to love to hike the Grand Canyon. I have friends who have hiked it at least once a year for a decade. One of them gets his daily protein from dry milk made palatable by this sauce, used many ways.

1/2 cup instant dry milk
3 tablespoons whole wheat flour
1/4 teaspoon salt
1 shake cayenne pepper
1 packet Butter Buds
2 cups water

Mix together in saucepan or skillet, stirring and heating slowly until smooth and thick. Then, to beat menu monotony:

● Stir in 1/4 cup cubed cheese and bacon bits, or slices of salami, to serve over biscuits.

● Stir in tuna and freeze-dried vegetables.

● Add grated cheese, and pour over pasta or rice.

● Add chunky chicken from a can, and serve over corn bread or biscuits.

(Butter Buds come in a box of foiled packets, an all-natural powder with the flavor of butter . . . almost.)

Olé Turkey Mole

Turkey Mole, or turkey in a spiced chocolate-chile sauce sounds complicated. I backed off trying it until my husband and I visited the Ramon Caballero family at San Carlos Bay in Mexico. "Mole is easy," I was told. "You just cook the turkey in a soup pot, then save the stock and brown the turkey chunks. Bake the meat in the sauce." It works, and it is a truly southwestern way to have Thanksgiving turkey on the desert or patio.

Buy 5 to 7 pounds turkey parts; thigh and breast are best. Simmer until tender with onion, carrot, a bouquet garni, and a little salt in water to cover. Discard bones and skin.

Brown turkey chunks in sunflower oil, salting lightly, transferring to Dutch oven. In browning skillet, make Mole Sauce.

2 tablespoons oil
5 ounces slivered almonds
4 tablespoons sesame seeds
2 teaspoons crushed dry red pepper
1/2 cup chopped onion
1/2 cup green chile pepper (minus seeds)
4 garlic cloves, minced
8 pimentos, chopped
2 garlic cloves
Pinch of anise seed
1 teaspoon vanilla
4 ounces melted Mexican chocolate
  (or 4 ounces semisweet chocolate
  with 1 tablespoon cinnamon)
3 tablespoons tomato paste
1/4 cup masa harina
4 cups turkey broth

To oil in browning skillet, add 2 tablespoons oil, then brown almonds, sesame seeds, and red chile pepper. Add onion and green chile pepper, 4 cloves minced garlic, and pimentos. Then blend in additional garlic, anise seed, vanilla, and melted chocolate. Combine chocolate-chile mixture with tomato paste, masa, and turkey broth. Pour over meat. Bake covered, about 2 hours at 350 degrees, until turkey is very tender and sauce is thick.

Serve with tortillas, beans, and rice (cooked separately and seasoned to taste), corn on the cob, and mixed green salad. Mole is even better reheated. This amount serves 10 to 12, depending on side dishes.

Albert's Pesto Supreme

"We eat on the patio, porch, or the balcony. We love to look at the Mogollon Rim straight away, through the pines," Al Saraceno enthused. He and wife Jimmie Ruth "retired" to Pine, sometimes sharing cooking duties. Jimmie Ruth writes, teaches Tonto Apache cooking classes, and dries herbs and flowers. Al once supervised landscaping at Scripps Institute of Oceanography, and grows the herbs and vegetables they use so well. His pasta salad with pesto sauce is a meal you can enjoy outside . . . with a Rim view or not.

2 cups fresh basil leaves
3 cloves garlic
1/3 cup pine nuts or walnuts
1/2 cup each, olive oil
  and fresh-grated
  Parmesan cheese

Place basil leaves, garlic, and pine nuts in blender or processor and pulverize. Add oil and blend until smooth. Add cheese and blend briefly. Refrigerate.

Serve over fresh pasta, especially fettuccine. Cold pasta makes a magical salad, coated with just a little pesto sauce, then tossed with fresh mushrooms, ripe olives, tomatoes, green or red bell pepper chunks, and even diced leftover meat. Or drizzle pesto over baked potato, green beans, tomatoes, summer squash, or fresh corn with peppers. Delicious, every one.

Chill Factor Avocado Blend

Ethel Hulbert Renwick, now of Carefree, wrote *A World of Good Cooking* after making three trips around the world. It became a Simon & Schuster best seller. Then she wrote two nutritional books based on concern about additives. "Food is the only cell-building option we get," she wrote. "A poor diet builds defective cells. Real cell-building food is wonderful." Her Avocado Blend is a soup, as given, but becomes a sauce or a salad dressing when thinned. All of these add cell-building chill factors during 100-degree weather. Easy patio fixing.

> 2 medium ripe avocados
> 1 cup chicken broth
> 1 cup yogurt or cream
> Sea salt to taste

Blend all ingredients until very smooth in blender. Chill. Serve in soup cups, garnished with very thin lemon slices.

Thin with olive or canola oil to use as dressing over hot or cold steamed vegetables. Thin further to use as salad dressing.

(OPPOSITE PAGE) *Sometimes "outdoor cooking" involves no cooking at all. Salsa cruda, the uncooked salsa favored by many southwestern cooks, can be prepared easily with nothing more than a sharp knife and carefully washed ingredients — usually chiles, tomatoes, garlic, and onions — plus seasonings.*

A Sauce for Roasted Meats

Sauces were used by Indians, too. This one was told to me by a Comanche friend. Most game, except for bear, is lean and cooks dry. Take equal parts of wild honey, water, and tallow. When you remove roast from the fire, brush this sauce over the meat at once and serve.

Mushroom Comfort Sauce

This can be made of wild mushrooms and wild onions, if you have your mushroom book along — and take no chances. One bite of the wrong mushroom is one bite too many. This yummy sauce can be thinned to soup or cuddled to noodles — even with burgers or steak.

> 2 tablespoons butter
> 2 tablespoons good oil
> 2 cups fresh mushroom slices and bits
> 1 cup diced onions and a few tops
> 1/4 cup flour
> 2 to 3 cups milk
> 1/2 teaspoon salt
> 1/4 teaspoon cayenne pepper

Heat butter and oil in a 2-quart saucepan, then sauté onions and tops with mushrooms. Carefully stir in the flour over low heat. One cup at a time, add milk, stirring as you go. As sauce thickens, add salt and cayenne. Keep heat low and allow sauce to simmer and pick up flavor. Super with meat, chicken, pasta, fish, ham.

Cherry Ham Glaze

The Fourth of July, or any picnic celebration, calls for ham. Dot Sydnor came up with a glaze as colorful as the sunsets behind Camelback Mountain.

1-pound can
   cherry pie filling
1 cup orange marmalade
1 teaspoon
   finely grated orange rind
1/4 teaspoon liquid smoke
1/2 cup sherry or
   sherry flavoring
1 9- to 10-pound ham

Heat juice from pie filling (reserving cherries) with marmalade, orange rind, liquid smoke, and sherry to make glaze. Have ready-to-eat ham cut in half for better balancing on the spit. Score fat in diamond pattern. Run spit through the ham, each half on a separate spit fork for better balance, and start rotisserie motor. Allow 10 minutes cooking per pound. Brush glaze over ham the last 20 minutes, applying generously. Garnish with warmed cherries to serve.

Don's Mustard Sauce

Picnics and potlucks along with spirited meetings united homeowners in the Encanto Park district of Phoenix as they forged a citizens association for scenic and historic preservation. Don Harding's mustard sauce works for any picnic.

1 2-ounce can Coleman's dry mustard
1/2 cup vinegar
3/4 cup sugar
2 eggs

Mix dry mustard and vinegar and let stand in a glass bowl, covered, overnight. Cook slowly with sugar and lightly beaten eggs over a double boiler. Stir often to bring to desired consistency, about 45 to 60 minutes thickening time. For a vegetable dressing, add to mayonnaise. For a vegetable dip, add curry powder to taste. Yield: a shy pint.

McCleve's Steel Etcher Salsa

Michael McCleve, Arizona sculptor, transforms welded steel and iron into surreal iconic and polychromed works. "I make two versions of salsa. You can serve one at a debutante ball, or upgrade it for a raiding party of mercenaries. Steel Etcher is for genteel folks," McCleve promises.

1 pound can peeled tomatoes
6 fresh green onions with tops
2 dozen assorted fresh chile peppers
1 tablespoon peppercorns, ungrated
2 tablespoons ground cumin
1 tablespoon sage
2 tablespoons garlic powder
1 tablespoon oregano

Halve and split vegetables, except for tomatoes, which are poured into a blender with their juice. Pack into blender the onions and assorted peppers (anchos, serranos, fresnos, and a few jalapeños, according to degree of picante desired). Blend on frappé setting, adding seasonings. Process to thick, not chunky stage.

If you take this salsa camping, keep it in the icebox, tightly capped. Makes 2 pints.

Dorothee's Kahlúa Kabobs

Dorothee Polson literally traveled the world for more than 20 years as a food writer with *The Arizona Republic*. She says, "None of my cherished recipes are so-called 'gourmet cooking,' whatever that means." Nevertheless, her recipes are a bit unusual, and this chutney-Kahlúa sauce is a memorable example.

1/2 cup chutney
1/4 cup coffee-flavored liqueur
1 tablespoon soy sauce
1 tablespoon vinegar
3 tablespoons salad oil
1/2 teaspoon coarse-ground pepper

Mince or mash your favorite chutney. Combine it thoroughly with liqueur — Kahlúa or your version of coffee liqueur. Add soy sauce, vinegar, oil, and pepper. Put all ingredients into blender and process at high until thick and smooth. To use, have ready 4 pounds lean pork loin, cut into 1 1/2-inch cubes. Alternate on skewers with strips of green pepper, whole pimentos, parboiled onions, and fresh pineapple chunks. Grill kabobs 20 minutes, then brush with sauce every few minutes until tender. Makes eight bronze-glazed portions.

Aioli Sauce

Garlic defenders love Aioli sauce — named for its pungent ingredient and loaded with it. What better time to indulge your taste for the bud or the clove than at any outdoor event?

6 crushed garlic cloves
2 egg yolks at room temperature
1/2 cup olive oil
1/2 cup vegetable oil
1/2 lemon, freshly squeezed
Salt and pepper to taste

Rinse a mixing bowl or blender jar with warm water. Add garlic, begin beating, and add the egg yolks. Continue beating, adding oil, a few drops at a time at first, then in a slow, steady stream until all is absorbed. Add lemon juice. Taste, then add salt and pepper as desired. Yield: 1 cup.

This sauce keeps a week refrigerated and *well* covered, but keep chilled until serving time. Use with any one or an array of seafood, shellfish, and vegetables. Vegetables may be raw, steamed, or boiled, served warm or cold. Try little red potatoes, artichokes, beets, leeks, green beans, pea pods, zucchini, garbanzo beans, or carrots. They all chum up with garlic.

Easy-way Show-stopper Sauces

Fix-ahead favorites for wise hosts and hostesses mean they enjoy outdoor entertaining as much as their guests. Here are some little glamour sauces to use again and again.

Fruited Amaretto Sauce

Sheila Shelor makes cooking fun. "This dessert leads to dawdling, savoring every bite," she says. Perfect after a grilled meal on the patio.

3 cups fresh berries or peaches
4 tablespoons Amaretto liqueur
4 tablespoons powdered sugar

Toss fruit lightly with Amaretto and sugar. Serve with this sauce: 8 ounces ricotta cheese, 8 ounces cream cheese, 1/2 cup sugar, 4 egg yolks, 2 tablespoons heavy cream, and 3 tablespoons Amaretto. Blend until smooth. Pour over fruit and serve at once, to six. A dessert and after-dinner drink in one, it's just the right comrade for coffee.

(RIGHT) Incredibly simple but indescribably tasty, Fruited Amaretto Sauce enhances fresh fruit as an after-dinner coffee companion on the patio.

Rhum Coconut Sauce

Frank Niemiec's favorite foods are Polish; his wife, Annie's, are Filipino. In this island recipe, only the butter is Polish.

8 tablespoons sugar
1 grated orange rind
1/2 cup fresh-grated coconut flakes
1/2 tablespoon butter
1/2 cup rhum (Annie's spelling)

Heat all ingredients in small pan, stirring well. Pour over crepes folded into four, and flambé at table. What tastes better than a delicate crepe in blazing sauce under the stars?

Easiest-ever Hollandaise

DeDe Meyers turns out this happy Hollandaise.

1/4 pound butter, room temperature
3 or 4 egg yolks
2 tablespoons lemon juice
Salt and cold water, sometimes

Place yolks in heavy saucepan over low heat. Add butter. Beat with mixer until set. Add lemon juice, beating into mixture until very smooth. If it becomes too stiff, carefully add a little *cold* water, never hot. Sometimes she adds salt; sometimes not. Makes enough to serve six to eight generously over grilled vegetables.

Apricot-mustard Sauce

Delightfully zany community volunteer Linda Pulaski forever surprises Tempe friends with easy-do wonders. Combine 1/2 cup apricot preserves with 2 tablespoons Dijon mustard. Terrific with crispy chicken or pork.

Notes

CHAPTER 8

Flour Power

Of course, there is outside bread. It started outside like all cooking — from mesquite beans ground to cakes and cooked on a stone, to slap bread (tortillas) and hearth bread to fry bread.

Nowhere, except in the Southwest, are you likely to encounter perfect Dutch oven biscuits and unforgettable Indian breads, both fry and horno-oven baked.

The original pioneer bread, the corn cake, is baked today heated with jalapeños. Suddenly, flour tortillas are the backpacker's and camper's friend — the easy, compact way to carry sandwich material.

A big deal in pizza is to grill the dough for fire-toasted flavor. Anything, from burger and hot dog buns to long torpedoes of yeast bread, is grilled and topped with cheese, chopped herbs, garlic, and seeds from poppy to sesame.

From do-ahead orange-chocolate-chip patio muffins to canned biscuit dough twisted around a stick to super-energy hiker breads like Logan and lead bread — we're in the dough.

(OPPOSITE PAGE) The basic Flour Power of Arizona may be called fry bread, Indian popovers, or squaw bread. By whatever name, it's delicious, and with the addition of refried beans, grated cheese, salsa, and other toppings, becomes the justly famous Navajo Taco.

Pioneer Flour Power

"How it used to be" is always the story-telling focus at the annual meeting of the Pioneer Stockman's Association. Peter Masse recalled: "In the early days, on a long ride, if you came to a camp or a house, you stayed, even if nobody was there. You fed your horse, cooked your dinner, and left everything as you found it. One time I stopped at a fellow's camp and looked in his Dutch oven. No food at all. A lady had a ranch about four miles beyond. He was there, but all she had was about 15 pounds of flour and half a pound of lard and some coffee.

"She fixed fry bread and I never had anything taste so good. When I left, the lady divided her flour and grease and coffee with this fellow and said something I never forgot: 'If you've got flour and grease, you're not out of grub.'"

— *Recorded by Roseanne and Marsha Carter*

Italian Bread on the Barbecue

"This is for desert eating in the hot, hot summer when the idea of using your oven is laughable," Sherri Springer of Mesa wrote me. "I've been a happy summer baker ever since I adapted this recipe from a *Sunset* article." Make the sponge a day ahead. It can be made the same day, but longer aging gives it the extra sour flavor.

  2 1/3 cups water, 110 degrees
  1 package dry yeast
  1 2/3 cups whole wheat flour
  1 teaspoon salt
  1 cup olive oil
  4 1/2 cups unbleached flour
  1 cup chopped fresh basil leaves
  3/4 cup chopped fresh oregano
  3/4 cup chopped fresh parsley
  Kosher salt

Sponge. Mix 1 2/3 cups of the warm water with yeast in large glass bowl. Let stand until yeast dissolves, 5 minutes. Stir in whole wheat flour and let stand overnight or at least 4 hours.

Bread. Add the remaining 2/3 cup water, 1 teaspoon salt, and 3 tablespoons of the olive oil, then begin to beat in the 4 cups of unbleached flour, a bit at a time. When dough pulls away from sides of the bowl, cover and let rise. Or chill overnight if desired.

Grill Time. Mix herbs into dough and knead to expel air bubbles. Divide into 6 balls. Cover dough when not working with it. On a lightly floured board, roll each ball into a 10-inch round, drizzle with olive oil, and sprinkle with kosher salt. Stack on a baking sheet with foil between the layers. Light the barbecue grill for medium heat. When ready, slide one bread dough at a time onto grill. Cook 5 minutes. Check for gold specks, flip and continue grilling until second side is lightly bronzed. Serve hot, warm, or cool. Guests have been known to seize the whole thing and go hide among the hibiscus until bread is devoured.

Fry Bread

Forget the Pillsbury Bake-Off. In Arizona the contest to see is a fry bread contest. It varies in name from one Indian tribe to another. In Sacaton, at the annual Mul-Chu-Tha, Pima ladies vie for prizes in a popover contest. At Window Rock, during the annual Navajo Tribal Fair, both men and women get elbow deep in flour while competing to win the fry bread title. At Sells, at the annual rodeo and fair on the Tohono O'odham Reservation, some years there is a fry bread contest and other years they just make and sell it. The Apaches' traditional loaf is ash bread, but they found that frying is quicker than baking in hot coals, so now they do both.

My first recipe came from Manuelita Lewis, who shepherded me through Mul-Chu-Tha as officials slapped down identical equipment for each contestant. Pretty basic stuff:

A pint enamel measuring cup; a red-and-white bowl big enough for mixing several pounds of popover dough; 1 long-handled fork; 1 large slotted spoon; 1 hot pad; an empty flour sack, and an aluminum lid to fit over the large iron fry pan.

Then and now, ingredients consist of: a 10-pound and a 5-pound sack of flour; a 1-pound box of lard; a blue box of salt, and an 18-ounce can of K.C. Baking Powder, all of them unopened.

Each contestant starts her own fire (no sissy stuff like chile contestants with their propane equipment), selecting her wood from a pile of split mesquite. Each woman is issued a length of iron with which to splinter the wood. Once the fire has burned to a steady heat, several plops of lard are spooned into the frying pan and left to melt, covered.

The basic recipe: 2/3 bowl of flour, mixed with 1 palmful of salt, plus 2 big pinches of baking powder. Work into this almost 1 cup of water. Knead until a smooth dough is fashioned. Pinch off small balls of dough and deftly slap them over palms and wrists into circles to fit the frying pan, allowing room for some expansion. Fry until golden on both sides, then fork out and drain.

Wheat Flour Tortilla Mix

Barbara Hernandez worked as an aide for the Maricopa County Extension Service, a helping arm of the University of Arizona's College of Agriculture. She taught families about food preparation and nutrition. This simple formula for Tortilla Mix is the easy way to make a quantity of flour tortillas to use a dozen ways — for patio or picnic food, hiking quickies, or handmade burro sandwiches.

10 cups all-purpose flour
1 cup powdered milk
2 tablespoons salt
1 1/2 cups shortening

Combine dry ingredients and mix well. Cut in shortening with two knives until mix is the consistency of coarse cornmeal. (Many cooks still use pure lard.) Store in container with very tight lid.

To make tortillas, combine 4 cups of mix with 1 cup lukewarm water. Stir well. Knead on lightly floured surface for 50 strokes. Form into 12 balls with floured hands. Cover balls with clean cloth. Heat ungreased griddle or big iron fry pan or top of wood stove. Tortillas are best if dough stands a half-hour before rolling.

Pat one dough ball at a time into a circle, then flatten with a floured rolling pin to make a 12-inch tortilla. Experienced tortilla cooks can pat large, very thin, almost translucent circles with hands alone, but the rolling pin does a good, fast job. Cook dough on medium hot surface (not hot-hot) until bubbles pop up, then turn and cook other side until light toasty brown. Cover with a clean towel, stacking as all 12 are cooked. If not wolfed down, wrap and freeze.

Grandad's Scratch Biscuits

Bud Brown came to Arizona as a Dartmouth grad. He fell in love with Isabelle, whose father, Ross Fuller, owned a ranch near Pine. Ross taught Bud how to ranch and raise horses and, just as important, gave him lessons in Dutch oven biscuits. When ranching was depressed, Bud taught school so well he won a National Golden Key Award in 1971. (Joan Ganz Cooney, one of his students, insisted he share her honors for creating *Sesame Street*.) The Browns founded Friendly Pines Camp for kids in Prescott. In 1990, they observed their 60th wedding anniversary with throngs of friends. No time to make his biscuits, so he gave me the recipe. Well, the method . . .

"Grandad's Scratch Biscuits, usually made in a bowl-shaped hollow found in the top part of a sack of flour (Yes, Virginia, flour and sugar once were sold in cloth sacks exclusively) followed no real recipe, but were the world's best. Into the 'bowl' went what he judged was the right amount of canned milk and water, along with salt, sugar, and baking powder measured, by sight only, and gently stirred round and round to mix well and start absorbing flour from the walls of the 'bowl.'

"As his mixture thickened, Grandad rolled it into a ball — never stirring — until it was thick enough to handle without sticking to his floured right hand. The left hand was never involved in the dough and always kept clean to handle the gancho (a metal hook used with

Dutch ovens).

"Meanwhile, the oven lid was getting hot on the fire as it burned down to make the coals. The oven itself, sitting on the lid, had been getting warm, not hot. If it melts lard or Crisco slowly without smoking, it is just right. It may have to be removed before you're ready to load it. Set it on a rock or firewood, not damp or cold ground, lest it crack. Even more forcibly, the rule goes for a hot lid, which should never touch the ground.

"Grandad, working from the flour sack, next pinched off hunks of dough. Squeeze and toss each a few times, *right hand only*; dip both sides in the puddle of shortening on the low side of the oven, and fill it, outside circle first, into center.

"Your good hardwood fire has burned to red coals. Handy by, scoop a shallow depression slightly larger than your oven. Fill the depression with ashes and coals (ashes act as insulator) and place oven on top. Skim off hot coals, with *no* ashes, to cover the lid (lid straight down, no crack for heat to escape).

"Most new cooks get too much heat on the bottom, not enough on top. Don't forget to give your hot oven a half turn every five minutes to even the heat, also rotating the lid when you peek at your biscuits. In about 20 minutes, biscuit heaven. Wrap in foil to keep warm, fry bacon (ditto), and make delicious gravy in bacon drippings. Pour coffee, and *bon appétit!*"

Biscooks

Jean Vaughn wrote the dedication poem which prefaces the *Pleasant Valley Homemakers Cookbook*. My favorite two lines salute the women who brought the Pleasant Valley War to an end:

"We'd rather eat than fight, they said.
"We'd rather be full of food than lead."

Biscooks, too, have no relationship with lead. They're healthy.

2 cups whole wheat flour
1 cup wheat germ
3/4 teaspoon salt
2 teaspoons baking powder
Milk
4 tablespoons vegetable cooking oil

Mix dry ingredients thoroughly. Add cooking oil and cut into dry mixture. Begin adding from 3/4 cup milk slowly, first mixing with a spoon, then kneading, until only enough has been added to make dough hold together. Roll out dough on board until 1/4 inch thick. Cut out with biscuit cutter. Bake in iron skillet over coals, like scones. Or, bake in 400-degree oven 18 minutes or so until tops are golden and crisp. Makes two-dozen winners.

(OPPOSITE PAGE) "Grandad" knew what he was doing when he made his Scratch Biscuits in a Dutch oven. Now, thanks to Bud Brown's generous recollections, the rest of us do, too.

Biscuits on a Stick

The quickest way to biscuits, and as much fun as marshmallows, are biscuits on a stick baked over coals or fire. It's safe, too, for all but the youngest. Mix a couple of cups of biscuit mix with a tablespoon of oil (or warm butter) and enough water to make a soft dough, about a half-cup. Pinch off pieces to make long, hot-dog-roll biscuits. Wrap around a 1-inch stick or dowel that has been soaked a few minutes or oiled, or both. Be sure dough covers the end of the stick. Slowly turn over coals until golden brown With care, pull hot, long biscuit off stick. Fill hole with butter and jam, squeeze cheese, or a little maple syrup. Enough dough for 8 biscuits on a stick.

Camp Biscuits with Daisies

Frank Reid's Camp Biscuit recipe appeared in a Flagstaff Methodist Church cookbook printed in the early 1900s. Frank, a sheepherder, had the cooking soul of a poet.

"Take a good deal of flour, more or less, according to the number of biscuit eaters and dimensions of their appetites, to which add salt 'to taste' and baking powder 'to raise.' Mix with water into a soft dough, bake in a Dutch oven, frying pan, or whatever utensil may be at hand — using a flat stone, if nothing else can be found. Serve hot on a tin plate or piece of bark, garnished with pine cones and field daisies."

Stuffed French Toast

Petie and Ray Bartram are noted for serving the biggest and most unusual bed-and-breakfast wake-up meals in the Lakeside area, maybe in the state.

    1 loaf French bread
    1 8-ounce package cream cheese
    2 tablespoons jam
      or frozen citrus concentrate
    3 or 4 eggs
    1/2 cup cream
    1 teaspoon vanilla
    1 teaspoon sugar

Slice bread lengthwise, not all the way through. Blend cream cheese and jam or concentrate. Spread on cut sides of bread and press the halves together. Refrigerate several hours or overnight. Slice and dip in batter made with eggs, cream, vanilla, and sugar. Grill until golden brown on griddle or on nonstick pan sprayed with Pam. Best done under ponderosa pines or at the patio grill. For guests who need low-cal food, make this with egg substitute, skim milk, and sugar substitute. They'll love it.

Blue Corn Chile Bread

On the Hopi Indian Reservation, blue corn is most used for piki bread, but it makes an unforgettable cornbread when teamed with jalapeño peppers and lots of cheese.

    1 1/2 cups fine blue cornmeal
    1/2 cup all-purpose flour
    1/2 teaspoon salt
    1 tablespoon baking powder
    1 cup chopped onion
    1 cup milk or sour milk
    1/2 cup melted butter
    4 jalapeño peppers, chopped
    1 1/2 cups grated cheese

Mix together cornmeal, flour, salt, baking powder, and onions. Add milk and melted butter. Mix well. Pour half the batter into a greased 8- by 12-inch baking pan. Place half the cheese over the batter, then evenly spread the finely chopped peppers, then the remaining cheese. Cover with remaining batter and bake 1 hour at 350 degrees. Or cook 40 minutes in Dutch oven, or 30 minutes over the coals in a cast-iron skillet, covered most of the time. Makes nine generous servings.

OPPOSITE PAGE) *Cooked in whatever's handy — baking pan, Dutch oven, or cast-iron skillet — Blue Corn Chile Bread is hard to forget.*

Coffee Can Bread

When coffee started to come in cans, grandma found herself with a new supply of cooking utensils. Alberta Hubbell updated this recipe for members of the Pine-Strawberry Homemakers Club.

1 package dry yeast
1/2 cup warm water
1/2 teaspoon ginger
3 tablespoons sugar
1 can evaporated milk, warm
2 tablespoons oil
1 teaspoon salt
4 to 4 1/2 cups flour
2 coffee cans, 1-pound size

Dissolve yeast in warm water in a large bowl. Blend in ginger and 1 tablespoon of the sugar. Let stand until it bubbles, about 15 minutes. Stir in the other 2 tablespoons sugar, then the milk, oil, and salt. With wooden spoon, beat in flour, 1 cup at a time, using enough to make a soft dough. Grease coffee cans well. Divide dough into cans. Cover with plastic lids, if available, or cloth napkin. When lids pop off (or dough humps higher than can's rim), bake in a 350-degree oven for 45 minutes. Cool on rack before removing can so bread will not crack. Erna Blatt bakes hers in coals for 30 minutes, removes cautiously, and retained heat finishes bread. Cans may be reused.

Logan Bread

"Pack it light" is the hiker's, climber's, and backpacker's principle. Logan Bread is about as heavy as bread can be — nutritious and indestructible, too. The original Logan Bread was conceived by a Fairbanks, Alaska, baker (no doubt second cousin to a brick mason) for a 1950 climb of Mt. Logan in the Yukon. Dozens of versions have followed.

Adding iron to your diet is the idea behind the bread. An iron deficiency alters thyroid metabolism, which controls body heat. An orange or vitamin C taken with this increases iron absorption. Keep a chunk handy if you wake up cold.

1 cup rye or rice flour
2 cups white flour
3 cups whole wheat flour
2 1/2 cups oatmeal (not instant)
1 cup chopped dried apricots
1 cup raisins, unsulphured
1 1/2 cups brown sugar
3 teaspoons baking powder
1/2 cup powdered milk
1 cup molasses
1 cup canola oil
1/2 cup honey
1 cup soy grits
6 eggs
2 teaspoons sea salt

Combine all ingredients in very large bowl and mix. Spoon-pour into four 9 by 9-inch greased pans. The idea is to bake brownie-like energy bars. Bake 45 minutes at 350 degrees. Because it's high in oil (some use part butter) this recipe turns out cakes that don't look quite done but turn solid as they cool. When cold, slice into 4-inch squares and wrap each in plastic wrap or foil. Logan Bread will give you, per square, about 600 calories and 9 grams of usable protein.

Pon (Camp Bread)

The First Families of Arizona were organized in 1932 and have celebrated with more than 50 years of outdoor parties since. Albert E. Harer Sr. wrote out this recipe for lip-smackin' Dutch oven bread for their *Recipe Roundup*. His directions obviously are those of a no-fooling, qualified camp veteran.

> 2 cups unsifted flour
> 2 teaspoons baking powder
> 1 teaspoon salt
> 4 slices bacon in crisp bits
> 1/4 cup bacon drippings
> 1 cup milk, approximately

Mix dry ingredients. Fry bacon and add grease to flour mixture, then add broken bacon by cutting in. Add enough milk to make heavy paste. Scrape dough on floured board and turn once or twice. Press into well-greased Dutch oven, turning once to grease all sides. Bury entire Dutch oven in hot coals. Bake 20 to 30 minutes until golden brown.

(OPPOSITE PAGE) *The campfire or barbecue grill can warm up already prepared foods, such as French bread. Doctored with butter and garlic and wrapped in foil, it gently warms while the cook creates the main course.*

Greenhouse Mesquite Muffins

Experienced desert hikers like to glean something for the pack. The mesquite bean, properly treated, is worth getting to know. My lessons came from Ruth Greenhouse, research associate at the Phoenix Desert Botanical Garden. To make mesquite pod flour, pick fully ripe beans from trees in the fall. Check for beetle holes. Clean and heat beans in 170-degree oven 4 hours — or sun dry — to destroy possible internal parasites. Grind into flour, which is so sweet you need no additional sugar. Mix 2/3 cup of mesquite flour with 1 1/3 cups self-rising (a must) flour. Beat 1 egg, 1/4 cup vegetable oil, and 3/4 cup milk to a froth. Add to flours and stir just until moistened. Pour into well-greased, 12-muffin pan, 2/3 full. Bake 25 minutes at 400 degrees. Cool, remove, munch, and dream of your desert walk.

Notes

Chapter 9

Dessert Me — Please!

Very few outdoor cooks ignore dessert. Those who loftily denounce brownies or carrot cake will admit a touch of something sweet tops off a fresh-air meal — maybe an apple. Some do take a bit of chocolate — strictly for energy, of course.

Dessert is adapted from the French *disserve*, meaning to clear away. They made a ceremony of serving oranges and apples, nature's tooth polishers, a splendid idea. My favorite outdoor sweets are those incredibly flavorful rubies in the grass, wild strawberries — and plump, sun-warmed huckleberries picked from the bush.

Wild sweets, however, only become cookbook material when a grill-glaze, a biscuit-dough topping, or a chewy crust further enhances the fruit.

By now, through the magic of reconstitution, puddings and cobblers; lo, even ice cream, can be brought to life in the wilds. (Don't forget a packet of spices and dried orange peel, though.)

Listed here for the tailgate, patio, and picnic crowds are surprising outdoor treats that urge us to say "Dessert me, please!"

(OPPOSITE PAGE) *There is no reason to neglect dessert, when such delicacies as lemon tarts garnished with violets can be part of a patio luncheon or dinner.*

Civil War Cake

"I first tasted this yummy, moist cake while backpacking in the Grand Canyon. It holds together well for carrying in a pack or saddlebag," explains Kelley Sullivan of Camp Verde. "They say it originated during the Civil War when there was a shortage of eggs."

Boil together 5 minutes, then let cool:
  1 pound raisins
  2 cups sugar
  2 cups water
Sift together:
  3 cups flour
  1 teaspoon each, salt, cinnamon, cloves
  1/2 teaspoon nutmeg

Add cooled raisin mixture to dry ingredients. Mix thoroughly. Add 1 teaspoon soda dissolved in a little water. Stir until blended in and the mixture froths a touch.

Pour into 2 deep metal loaf pans, 3 1/2 by 8 by 2 1/2, greased and floured. Bake 45 minutes at 375 degrees. Cake is done when top jumps back if lightly pressed with finger. Raisins will burn if you don't cover top of cake with foil after about half baked. Turn out on rack to cool. Wrapped in foil, cake stores in refrigerator for several weeks if no cowboys drop in.

Shoofly Cake

This dense, almost indestructible picnic cake goes back to its Pennsylvania roots in my life. Not too much molasses, just crumbly enough, a slab of this makes a cold day warm and a mug of the worst coffee taste like Arbuckle's best. Yet it buddies comfortably with icy, fresh-squeezed, puckery lemonade.

  4 cups flour
  2 cups sugar
  1 cup butter or margarine
  1/2 teaspoon salt
  1 cup molasses
  2 cups very warm water
  1 teaspoon soda

Mix flour, sugar, shortening, and salt until crumbly. Set aside 1 cup for topping. Mix molasses with warm water into which the soda has been stirred. It will foam a little. When it settles down, mix well into flour crumbs. Dough will be fairly thick. Grease and flour 13 by 8 by 2 pan. Oven should be preheated to 350 degrees. Pour cake dough into pan. Sprinkle crumbs evenly over top. Bake 45 minutes to an hour or when inserted toothpick emerges clean. My mother called this "toothache cake." If it seems too sweet, reduce sugar by a half-cup. Never gave me a toothache. Serves 12 to 15.

No-fail Fiesta Cake

I had just finished perfectly cooked salmon, so fresh I thought I was anchored off Vancouver Island. Actually, I was in Cave Creek. Mary Hirsch served this cake, and I'm no more likely to forget it than the salmon and the setting — a patio cut so skillfully into the desert that wild little critters and birds kept joining our luncheon. Try this. Impress somebody.

    1 1/2 cups flour
    1 cup sugar
    1/4 teaspoon salt
    1 teaspoon soda
    1 egg, beaten
    1 can (1 pound) fruit cocktail
    1 cup brown sugar
    1 cup chopped nuts

Sift together flour, sugar, salt, and soda. Add beaten egg and fruit cocktail, juice included. Blend well. Pour into greased 8 by 12 cake pan. Sprinkle top with brown sugar and nuts. Bake at 350 degrees for 45 minutes. Serve warm or cold. Option: Top with whipped cream. "My mother's golden oldie," Mary said.

Navajo Sprout Cake

Navajo women traditionally take full charge of the home and the sheep. They do the butchering and the cooking, much of it outdoors. In addition to morning fry bread, they used blue corn in breads and other dishes long before New Age advocates discovered it. Like the Hopi, the Navajo, too, use sprouted grains. This cake is guaranteed to sustain you through magical Monument Valley.

Bring 6 cups of water to a boil. Stir in 4 cups of blue cornmeal mush. Add 2 cups of yellow cornmeal mush. (Note, the meal has been cooked in both cases.) Stir in 1/2 cup brown sugar and 1/2 cup raisins, heaped. Slowly blend in 1 cup of sprouted wheat. Pour into greased baking pan, large and deep. Cover and bake slowly at 250 degrees for 4 hours, a must. Cool, cut into squares, and serve.

Fenzl Fancy Cookie Tacos

The old-fashioned taco was never like this. Fancy Cookie Tacos have the same familiar shape, but the filling is much more fanciful.

Dynamic Barbara Fenzl juggles chairmanship of Arizona's chapter of the American Institute of Wine and Food with ownership of Les Gourmettes Cooking School, both made-to-order sources for her job as food editor of *Phoenix Home & Garden*. When she and husband Terry entertain on the patio, guests expect and get a dessert as terrific as chocolate-fruit Cookie Tacos.

> 1 cup sugar
> 3/4 cup blanched almonds
> 1/4 cup water
> 1 quart vanilla ice cream
>   or flavor of choice
> Assorted colorful, ripe fruit,
>   cut in bite-size pieces

Place sugar and almonds in blender or food processor with steel blade. Grind very fine, then add water and mix well. It should be a paste. Let stand for 10 minutes. Preheat oven to 375 degrees. Line cookie sheets with parchment paper, and spoon half-dollar-size rounds onto paper, leaving about 4 inches between the cookies. Bake 10 to 13 minutes, or until evenly browned, in top half of oven, 1 tray at a time. Cut with scissors between the cookies, and gently fold edges of the paper to make 1 cookie a taco shape. Place it between 2 boxes of kitchen wrap until set, about 30 seconds. Quickly shape all the cookies; once they cool they cannot be bent without breaking.

Mexican Chocolate Sauce. Break 8 ounces good quality semisweet or bittersweet chocolate into small pieces. Add 1/4 cup strong coffee, 4 tablespoons heavy cream, and 1/4 teaspoon cinnamon. Heat over low heat in a small, heavy saucepan until chocolate is melted, stirring occasionally. Whisk until smooth.

Gently spoon small scoops of ice cream into each taco shell. Place fruit on top of ice cream and drizzle with chocolate sauce. Serves eight.

Carob Coconut Cookies

Although the world teems with chocoholics, there are many who distrust or are allergic to the richness of the cocoa bean. Carob is a worthy substitute. According to my friend Dee Kell, a nutritional adviser, carob has 2 percent fat in contrast to chocolate's 52 percent. It tastes only faintly like chocolate, but take cheer in its minerals and nutrients.

1 cup non-instant dry milk
1/2 cup carob powder
2/3 cup milk
1/2 cup honey
1 tablespoon almond extract
6 to 8 cups shredded coconut

Blend first 5 ingredients until smooth. Stir in coconut, even if part is freshly grated. Let dough sit 15 minutes so coconut absorbs moisture. Wet hands and shape into 1-inch balls. Bake on oiled cookie sheet at 350 degrees 12 minutes until light brown. Makes 2 dozen chewy cookies. A fine time to introduce yourself to carob is on a hike, when you are so starved that chick-peas taste like macadamia nuts.

1500s

"You can go a long way on these cookies," promises Ginger Allingham, who learned of their power while searching for foods to reinforce her Glendale Gauchos swim-team kids before a 1500-meter swim, or any other event demanding stamina.

1 cup whole wheat flour
1/2 teaspoon each, salt and soda
1 teaspoon cinnamon
1/2 teaspoon each, ginger and nutmeg
1/2 cup each, butter, brown sugar, and white sugar
1 egg
2 tablespoons milk
1 teaspoon vanilla
1 cup raisins
1 cup granola or oatmeal
1/2 cup each, wheat germ, coconut, and nuts

Mix together first six ingredients. Cream together in big bowl the next six ingredients. Add first ingredients. Mix together remaining goodies and add to dough. Drop by teaspoon on ungreased cookie sheets. Bake 12 to 15 minutes at 375 degrees. Makes 3 1/2 dozen power chews for human fish.

(OPPOSITE PAGE) *They may be the only cookies named for a swimming race. Ginger Allingham's 1500s are a nutritious free-style winner with a pitcher of milk under a grape arbor.*

Galletas de Cafe (Coffee Cookies)

Our first stop (after customs) on camping vacations to the Mexican beaches of Guaymas or Rocky Point was for bags of *galletas*. Mexican *panaderías* (bakeries) were a must. Then Socorro Munoz Kimble and Irma Serrano Noriega wrote one of Golden West's wonderful little cookbooks, *Mexican Desserts*. Here's their way to have a coffee break without the coffee pot or the bakery.

2 cups flour, sifted
2 tablespoons instant coffee
1/2 teaspoon salt
1 cup brown sugar
1 egg, lightly beaten
3/4 cup butter or margarine, melted

Preheat oven to 350 degrees. Combine flour, coffee, salt, and sugar in a bowl. Add egg and melted butter and mix well. On a lightly floured board, press dough to desired thickness; 1/4 inch is traditional. Cut in circles or favorite shapes. Bake on greased cookie sheets 20 to 25 minutes. Peek after 20 minutes; butter cookies can over-brown quickly at the end of baking time. Makes 2 dozen.

Traveling Fruit Cakes

Mildred Hooper, writer-photographer and history buff of Peoria, Arizona, originated this fruit-cake cookie, great little traveling companions to break out any time. The butter means they taste better with age — and they travel well in a pocket!

1 pound butter
1 pound light brown sugar
5 eggs
3 tablespoons milk
4 cups flour
1 teaspoon soda
1/4 teaspoon salt
1 pound white raisins
1 pound chopped nuts
1 1/2 teaspoons vanilla
1 cup flour
1 pound diced candied cherries
1 pound diced candied pineapple

Cream butter and sugar. Add eggs and milk. Sift flour with soda and salt. Stir into batter. Add raisins, which first should be steamed over hot water to plump. Blend in nuts and vanilla. Mix the cup of flour with diced fruit. Add to dough. Drop by teaspoon onto greased cookie sheets. Bake 12 to 15 minutes, depending on size, at 375 degrees. These remain moist and fragrant for several months. Yield: 12 dozen large or 24 dozen tea cookies.

Raspberry Dipped Fruit

Bill and Gail Meissner have become famous for their brunches, often ending with coffee and Raspberry Dipped Fruit.

Mix: 1/4 cup shredded coconut, 3 tablespoons chopped pecans, 1 cup sour cream, 1/4 cup raspberry preserves, and 2 tablespoons milk. Arrange fresh fruits of the season, sliced into fingers, around a bowl of this coconut raspberry dip on a bed of ice. Add a cup of fresh, slightly mashed raspberries to dip, when available. A relaxed, non-threatening way to end a hearty brunch or barbecue.

Dunkin' Platters

Mrs. Lars Nielson's traveling specials are these big, hearty cookies. They've traveled to and been dunked at school and church picnics, northern woodsy vacations, and camp.

Mix: 2 cups oil, 2 cups brown sugar, 2 cups white sugar, 4 beaten eggs, 2 teaspoons vanilla. Then add: 4 cups healthy flour, 2 cups each of cereal flakes and oatmeal, and 2 teaspoons each of baking soda and baking powder. Mix very well, then roll into balls, golf ball size. Bake on ungreased cookie sheets 8 to 9 minutes at 350 degrees. Makes about 175 2 1/2-inch cookies. Platters must never be overbaked. Chewy in the middle is right.

Let 'em Eat Dirt

B. J. Giffis ends her patio parties with her favorite dessert, Dirt. "I'm a freak for Oreo ice cream, which is not always available. So I use the food processor to crush a package of Oreo cookies and blend them with a half-gallon of quality vanilla ice cream," she explains. "It looks a lot like sandy soil. I serve it in little crocks or flower pots with a live daisy growing out of each."
 Voila! Great dirt!

Fruit 'n' Nut Crust

Stan Kelson founded the International Holistic Center in Phoenix and its satellite outdoor retreat in Strawberry. "People who don't know, think New Age food is dull. It is exciting and cleansing and health-giving and delicious," he says. "You bake bread by the sun, make milk and cheese from nuts and seeds, ice cream from fruit, and you exercise, exercise." Sounds almost easy when you're eating his Fruit 'n' Nut Crusted Fresh Strawberry Pie.

Knead together: 1 pound soft, pitted dates, 1/2 pound ground walnuts, and 3/4 cup shredded coconut. Press into 10-inch pie plate. Pour in fresh fruit filling. Easy and good for the whole family is a blend of 2 cups fresh, cleaned strawberries and 4 or 5 semi-frozen, very ripe bananas. Whirl to a soft, sunset pink. Do not exercise immediately after your serving.

Ginger Ice Cream

Mrs. Dick George, an oriental cooking whiz, made her own easy exotic Ginger Ice Cream because she couldn't find it anywhere. "Just soften a quart of quality vanilla ice cream, then put in the blender with 2 tablespoons diced, candied ginger. Blend well and refreeze. Serve in scoops, garnished with toasted almonds and flaked coconut."

Carrington Fresh Picked Cobbler

James Carrington "Bing" Brown has been a radio announcer, news reporter, photographer, and public relations executive and now operates his own communications company. Through it all, he built an enviable reputation as one of the state's Dutch oven magicians. "Remember," he says, "cooking should be done by intuition as much as by measurement. This is a guide, not the law."

1 1/2 cups fruit
1/2 to 2 cups water
3/4 to 1 1/2 cups sugar
2 cups Bisquick
1/4 pound margarine or butter
3/4 cup milk, canned or fresh
Lemon juice or vinegar, optional

Fresh picked berries, apples, apricots, cherries, or peaches work best. But Bing takes along canned fruit in case the birds or critters beat him to the fresh stuff. Whichever, make sure it's in bite-size pieces.

Bring the water to a boil and add the fruit, slowly adding sugar to your taste. If you oversweeten, adjust with lemon or vinegar. Continue to boil fruit until it is slightly softened. With canned fruit, use the syrup from the can with enough water to make 1 1/2 cups liquid. Then add fruit but do not continue to boil. Meanwhile, heat the Dutch oven in a good bed of burned-down hardwood coals.

Mix Bisquick, half the butter, and enough milk to make a dough of medium consistency. Bing rolls the dough into a long, thin shape (if it's easily pliable but barely stretches when held by one end, it's right). Divide into equal parts. Roughly shape like a thick pie crust, about the same diameter as the Dutch oven. Place the first piece of dough in the bottom of heated oven. Add the fruit mixture. Top with second dough and press down with a fork in several places so the crust isn't too even.

Put the top on the oven and the oven on the coals. Add other coals evenly to the top of the lid and a thin layer around the outside, between the oven and the cooking pit. In about 30 minutes, cobbler will be brown. Remove from heat and let cool 30 to 60 minutes. To serve, if you're feelin' fancy, and it's available, top each heaping, steaming plate with ice cream, whipped cream, or melted marshmallows. You're in Dutch oven heaven.

Saguaro Fruit Sundaes

Saguaro cactus fruit are ready to harvest when they turn a rich purple-crimson. If the birds are feasting greedily, take a plastic bucket, tongs, and gloves, and remove your share only. Fruit is clumped on the tips of saguaro arms; a bamboo pole, used gently, is helpful. (The Pima and Tohono O'odham Indians have always tipped off the plum-like fruit with dry saguaro ribs from fallen cactus.)

Wash fruit under running water in colander, and peel with a knife sharp enough for skinning. Spoon out the pulp, including the tiny black seeds. Sliced in half to reveal its ruby interior, a saguaro fruit looks amazingly like a bird-size watermelon. For each cup of pulp, add 1/4 cup of Chambord raspberry liqueur, mix lightly and refrigerate. To serve, alternate scoops of raspberry and vanilla ice cream with tablespoons of saguaro topping. Allow a slight melt to merge flavors and colors.

Fruit shells may be dried on trays or clean paper in full sun for 3 days. Good chewing and a fine mouth moistener on hikes.

Brunette Pears

Chocolate-topped pears bring applause anywhere. Always buy pears for the pack somewhat underripe. They continue to ripen if heat bakes them on the trail. Halve and remove centers and stems to grill, lightly oiling either the fruit or the grill. Allow several minutes per side over medium coals. Remove, shave a few curls of chocolate from a bar, arrange in favorite brunette hair style, and enjoy as it melts. For more elegant patio desserting, dress pears with syrup.

1 cup each, water and sugar
4 ripe pears
1/4 pound semisweet chocolate

Bring water and sugar to a simmer in a saucepan and cook to syrup, about 8 minutes. Peel, halve, and core pears and arrange, cut side down, in buttered baking pan or dish. Pour syrup over them and bake under cover on grill, about 20 minutes, turning and basting at least once. Turn out into shallow bowls and top with shaved chocolate while warm. Chocolate will shave easier if bar is warm or warmed between palms for a minute. Allow 2 halves per serving.

Sweet-tooth Brain Gain

Chances are, if you have a sweet tooth and feed it for outdoor energy, you're not so dumb. Researchers at the Massachusetts Institute of Technology discovered that a high-carbohydrate diet stimulates brain activity. The key is a chemical called serotonin that acts as a messenger between neurons, or information transmitter cells, in the brain. They did not infer, however, that a diet of brownies would make you an Einstein.

Notes

CHAPTER 10

Quenchers

Sangria to cocoa, hibiscus tea to sudden soups, let's drink to quenchers.

For campers and outdoor sportspersons, it is most often coffee. For hikers and climbers, it is tea and high-energy drinks. For summer picnickers, it is some form of mom's lemonade or amber-clear and ice-chunked sun tea.

Grillers and backyard chefs lean on the beer. Brunches begin with juices and punches, increasingly augmented with wine, vodka, and tequila. Trail punches include protein, fruits, and seasonings to disguise chemically treated water.

Soups, simple to gutsy, are mugging it everywhere, from first course on the patio while the fish grills to doubling as handwarmers when it rains in camp.

And instant breakfasts, mochas, and tea mixes should become part of your outdoor cooking strategy, too, as well as nutritious *atoles* (see page 127).

Water is the key. For strenuous outdoor pursuits, the body needs three to four quarts of refill a day (more in hot weather). Boiling or treating water has become a necessary way of back-country life. On the desert, the limiting factor is water, pure and simple.

(OPPOSITE PAGE) *So colorful, so refreshing, and tasty as all out-doors! Choose your delectable sip from Orange Julie, Hibiscus Tea Punch, Prickly Pear Punch, Luscious Lemonade, or Strawberry Plop Sangria.*

Hibiscus Tea Punch or Purifier

The warmer environs of this state are ideal for that vibrant, red- and yellow-hued showoff of the mallow family, the hibiscus. They enhance more than patio walls and gardens — that is, hibiscus flowers give tea or punch a rose-pink or a flame-orange tint and a pleasant tartness. You can wash fresh blossoms picked from your own bushes, tie the stems together, and hang to dry like herbs. Hikers and bikers use hibiscus in drinking water and canteens to offset the flavor of purifying tablets. For a refreshing, colorful tea or punch:

1 cup dried hibiscus flowers
1 quart boiling water
1/2 cup honey or sugar
**2 tablespoons fresh,
    strained lime juice**
1 quart white grape juice
2 cups orange juice
1 bottle white Zinfandel
1 cup cranberry juice

Tea. Steep flowers in boiling water for several hours or overnight to obtain color. For hot tea, add sweetener and lime juice. Remove flowers to reuse. Ice tea as usual.

Punch. Make tea with boiling water, flowers, and sweetener. When cool, add other ingredients. Serve in punch bowl with ice ring and lime slices. Float several fresh hibiscus blossoms on punch.

If you don't have hibiscus, high in vitamin C, in your backyard, the dried petals may be found in food co-ops and health food stores. Jeri Helms of Phoenix, an innovative nutritional cook, alerted me to jamaica (*hah-my-kah*), dried petals of wild red chrysanthemums from Mexico, available in border towns and import stores and useful for a similar punch or tea.

(OPPOSITE PAGE) *For a pleasantly tart flavor and a lovely color change, dried hibiscus blossoms can be steeped for tea. Hibiscus Punch is another winner, and for hikers, a few blossoms in drinking water offset the taste of purifiers.*

Earle's Prickly Pear Punch

For 20 years, W. Hubert Earle was the moving spirit of Phoenix's Desert Botanical Garden. At their desert home near Squaw Peak, he and his wife, Lucille, kept frozen prickly pear fruit juice on hand to refresh visitors.

2 cups prickly pear juice
1 quart limeade
1 quart ginger ale
1 juicy lime, thinly sliced
1 cup vodka, optional

Use tongs and gloves to pick red-mauve, ripe prickly pear fruit which round out late each summer. Fill a bucket. Transfer to large colander and wash under running water. Blanch for 1 minute in boiling water to soften skins and spines. All prickly pear fruit come armed with stickers, so spoon into blender with care. Puree enough fruit to make 2 cups, then strain through cheesecloth to make punch.

Blend well with limeade. (Some tastes may require a little sugar or honey.) Pour over ice block and, to serve, add chilled ginger ale. Garnish with lime slices. Punch is a clear, inviting, ruby-red color and the taste is bright. Recipe serves 20 to 24, depending on size of cup. Vodka mixes well with this juice, adding to taste. Additional fruit should be pureed and frozen.

Arizona Sun Tea

Visitors from space hovering over Arizona would wonder at all the jugs, filled with water and tea bags — turning amber by sun power — positioned on picnic tables, patio floors, and house steps. Sun tea is a way of life here — the clearest and tastiest thirst quencher we know, other than pure spring water.

For maximum pleasure, use shiny clean glass, never metal. Start with fresh, cold water, but not soft water.

1 gallon cold water
8 tea bags, one-serving size
Thinned honey sweetener
  to taste
Lemon, lime wedges or juice

Sterilize gallon jar. Add tea bags and water. Cover and place in full sunlight outdoors. Window tea is not the same. Bring inside when tea reaches desired color and strength. When cool, refrigerate. This tea will not cloud. My preference is orange-spice, which needs no sweetener. If sweetener is desired, add and stir into hot tea. (Recipe follows.)

Pour tea over the clearest ice you can find or make. Serve with lemon or lime wedges or their juice. Fresh is best.

Thinned Honey Sweetener
  1 cup local honey
  3 tablespoons warm water

Shake in jar (lid on) after stirring together to blend. Let stand, then shake again. Easily absorbed into tea, coffee, lemonade, and punches.

Doctor Mom's Luscious Lemonade

My introduction to Arizona lemonade came one May during the sneezin' season. A neighbor cheerfully told me that her kind of lemonade took care of allergies. "Local citrus gives you vitamin C and local honey is better than a shot to immunize you against our pollens," she promised. "I use this recipe for school and church punch. Enough for 40 kids, 10 teachers and parents, 2 cups each." Here is Doctor Mom's luscious prescription.

4 cups water
8 cups local honey (no other)
8 cups lemon juice
2 No. 2 1/2 cans unsweetened
  crushed pineapple
8 sliced navel oranges
4 gallons water
Ice, mint leaves, and lemon slices

Boil 4 cups water and honey 10 minutes. Cool resulting syrup. Add remaining ingredients and stir well. Use local citrus if possible. Serves 100.

The Crew's Sunshine Cooler

In the late 1960s, families moving into a new Tempe development called The Lakes adapted quickly to a lakeside lifestyle, boatnicking regularly. Soon there was a Woman's Club and a *Lakes Cookbook*, gathered during countless launchings and anchorings. Sunshine Cooler is a bubbly thirst-quencher for the whole family.

6-ounce can frozen lemonade
6-ounce can frozen orange juice
6-ounce can frozen limeade
4 cups cold water
1 quart lemon-lime seltzer
1 quart 7-Up, chilled

Combine all ingredients. Mix well and chill. Serves 12 to 15, according to Barbara Boyer, who gets just as thirsty playing tennis as trimming the mainsails.

(OPPOSITE PAGE) *Lemonade is lemonade is lemonade? Don't you believe it! Check Doctor Mom's recipe, then reduce the quantities if you're making it for a family picnic instead of a roomful of school kids.*

Immediate Satisfaction

Instant. The age of instant anything has resulted in a mix to match almost any product manufactured for the jiffy generation. And the mixes are always cheaper to make than to buy.

◆

Budget Bender Hot Chocolate Mix

8 cups non-instant powdered milk
1 cup sugar
1-pound can presweetened cocoa mix (like Quik)
1 6-ounce jar powdered nondairy creamer (like Pream)
Dash of salt

Combine all ingredients thoroughly (important), then store in a dry container, well sealed. To use, put one heaping spoonful in a mug filled with hot water. That's the way Evelyn Waldrip stirs it up when it's chilly in Young, Arizona.

Pat's Ski Tea

1/2 cup instant tea
1 cup sugar
2 cups powdered orange drink (Tang)
2 teaspoons or 1 packet powdered lemonade
1 teaspoon cinnamon
1 teaspoon cloves

Mix all ingredients well. Use 2 tablespoons in 1 cup of hot water. Spirits may be added if desired — rum, cider, red or rosé wine. This stores well indefinitely in an air-tight jar. "We think it's great on cross-country skiing or hunting trips," says energetic Pat Brock of Phoenix.

Spiced Mocha Mix

1 cup nondairy creamer
1 cup hot cocoa mix
2/3 cup powdered instant coffee
1/2 cup sugar
1/2 teaspoon ground cinnamon
1/2 teaspoon ground nutmeg

Mix together gently. Store in glass jar. To serve, add 3 or 4 heaping teaspoons of mix to a cup of boiling water. This spinoff from commercial coffee blends came from Karen Clements, Phoenix hostess who especially likes to serve outside "in the spring when the world is flowering."

◆

Frosted Root Beer

Red-haired Bessie Lipinski grew up in Jerome and became a schoolteacher who liked to make science lively with food experiments. The students' favorite was not a food, but a drink: ice-slushed root beer. Here's an easy way to cool down a crowd.

    5 gallons cold water
    5 pounds sugar
    6 ounces Hires Root Beer Extract
    5 pounds dry ice

Mix water, sugar, and extract in large container. A good choice is a big plastic tub, never a metal tub. (I saw an entire crowd felled by a vat of punch mixed with dry ice in a copper cauldron.) With this recipe the only other warning is: Handle dry ice with gloves while dropping it into center of mixture. Stir and watch the magic. When root beer gets slushy, dip and drink. This amount is supposed to serve 100 in small paper cups; but nobody wants a small cup.

Atole, Quick Corn Power

Atoles are a gift of Mexico, nurturing cornmeal drinks that are low-cost sources of energy, real beverage foods. This is the basic recipe. Campers can add an egg, fruit, or brewer's yeast for a quick breakfast or snack.

    1/2 cup cornmeal
    1/4 cup cold water
    2 cups salted, boiling water
    1 quart milk
    3 tablespoons brown sugar

Moisten cornmeal with cold water. Gradually add into the boiling, salted water, stirring until smooth and thick. Reduce heat. Simmer 15 minutes. Add milk and brown sugar. When hot and creamy, serve in cups or mugs. Serves five to six. Cinnamon sticks, ground cinnamon or nutmeg, or crushed anise seed may be added for a pleasant taste surprise.

Trail cooks sometimes make a version of this with hot cereals like Cream of Rice or Cream of Wheat, thereby gearing up fast and with no need to chew.

Homemade Instant Breakfast

In the early 1970s, Ellen Buchman Ewald's Tiger's Milk set off an explosion of thick protein drinks. Her recipe blended yogurt (which I think put yogurt on the path to today's popularity) with banana, honey, fruit juice, and brewer's yeast.

She said this about instant breakfast: "Expensive commercial instant breakfasts are mainly milk powder, flavorings, sugar, and chemicals which thicken and preserve. You can create your own flavors." Here is the simple way to drink breakfast after work or a swim, or on the trail.

    1 cup double milk (double in
        protein) made by using 1 cup
        cold milk and 1/4 cup
        powdered milk, or 1 cup
        water and 1/2 cup
        powdered milk

Blend with your choice:
1 tablespoon carob powder
1/4 teaspoon instant vanilla
Cinnamon to taste

1 teaspoon instant coffee
1 tablespoon honey
Cinnamon to taste

1 tablespoon Postum
1 tablespoon honey

1 tablespoon molasses
    or homemade preserves

1/4 teaspoon almond extract
1/4 teaspoon nutmeg
Honey to taste

Powdered Milk

Many recipes in this and most other outdoor pack-and-cook collections contain powdered milk. In every case, I suggest non-instant powdered milk. You can use and trust it in soups, cookies, breads, and sauces — even make good yogurt with it — skim or whole.

Instant powdered milk can turn bread and pudding to lead, can get stringy in sauces and yogurt, and doesn't have the nutritional value of non-instant. Still, when the tough need to get going, fresh milk *plus* powdered packs the most protein. Keep powdered mixes tightly sealed; bacteria can grow if moisture content increases. Beats leading a cow.

All-day Cup

Sonny Kitts served all around the world with the Navy, then worked at Fort Huachuca in southern Arizona. He never drove when he could walk, and explored everywhere. He could live out of a cup — a handy trick for most any hiker.

"A cup and spoon and a very light camping stove are all you need, except for light food. Enough cereal and dry milk and chocolate mix for several days, with instant soup and package stir-meals and fruit — that guarantees more time for walking and less for cooking," he grinned.

The cup should be big, easy to swirl clean (no grooves), and enamel-coated, cutting down on lip burns. For breakfast, boil water in the cup, add cereal and dry milk for extra protein, stir and eat clean. Follow with hot chocolate. Boil out with water. Soup for lunch, with fruit. Dinner? Heat macaroni with salami or instant potatoes with jerky and cheese, swirl with a splash of hot water, finish off with a final hot chocolate. Instant coffee granules can be added for the caffeine crowd. Now, if they'd just put Sonny to work on the national budget.

Hopi Milk Drink

"This is a fast drink with little or no sugar and a lot of vitamins and minerals," writes Juanita Tiger Kavena, author of the fascinating *Hopi Cookery* and a reservation home economist. There are no milk cows or goats on this tribe's high mesas, so powdered milk is the base, along with their unusual blue cornmeal.

1 cup powdered milk
5 3/4 cups warm water
1 cup finely ground
   blue cornmeal
3/4 cup cool water

Stir milk and warm water in saucepan until smooth. Over low heat, cook slowly 10 minutes, stirring to prevent scorching. In a small bowl, mix blue cornmeal with 3/4 cup of cool water, removing lumps. Stir cornmeal mixture into simmering milk. When well mixed, cook five minutes, stirring often. Add a little sugar or a dash of salt to taste. Adapted from an old recipe, this Hopi form of atole is used instead of cocoa or as a nighttime drink. Blue cornmeal is available at food co-ops, health food stores, and some supermarkets.

Orange Julie

Orange Julius, like Gatorade, achieved fame as a "health" drink, even though it usually washed down a big, steamed hot dog. Kimer Wadsworth came up with this facsimile of Julius. File this refresher to serve at your own hot dog roast.

2 cups orange juice
2 or 3 tablespoons sugar
1/2 cup milk
1/2 cup water
1 teaspoon vanilla
5 or 6 ice cubes

Whirl all ingredients in blender until creamy or foamy. Serves one 2-hot-dog person or two 1-hot-dog persons.

This recipe can be adapted for camping (minus the ice cubes) by using powdered orange drink and powdered milk, and by using a shaker instead of a blender. It loses a little in the translation but is a quick energizer.

Chris's Yogurt Serve

Early in Chris Evert's remarkable tennis career, as a mainstay of the professional Phoenix Racquets, she lived in Phoenix. Her after-practice pickup is a winner following any outdoor exercise, blended for cooling down on the patio.

1 ripe banana
1 cup milk
1 small container of yogurt,
    any fruit flavor

Freeze yogurt first. At serving time, mix frozen yogurt in the blender with sliced banana and milk about 40 seconds. "It's a delightful drink when you are hungry or thirsty but don't want too much of anything," Chris says. Sip slowly. Enough for two.

Quick Chill-quenchers

Camping weather can be so capricious, it is wise to mentally file no-frill ways to counter the chills.

An easy way to warm up with a gulp of iron-energy is to combine boiling water and blackstrap molasses. Or add blackstrap to hot coffee, tea, or milk. We health nuts slip in brewer's yeast.

Powdered lemon or orange drink mix sweetened with honey and a jot of ginger is every sip as refreshing hot as cold. Apple juice warmed with a flick of cinnamon is comfort on the trail.

Hot broth becomes an instant meal the oriental way by dropping in minced or dried vegetables swirled with an egg. Leftover rice or noodles freshened with chopped parsley and onion in hot broth is another satisfying quickie.

Chicken, beef, and vegetable cube or granule broths take on character with garlic, curry powder, herbs, or that lovable body warmer, ground chiles. Remember, the simple way to carry herbs and spices is in those flea-weight little plastic 35-mm film canisters.

Sudden Soups

With the help of cans and freeze-dried packages, soup is no longer an all-day project, unless you *want* to do a robust stew-soup in a Dutch oven or crockpot. If made at home, soups can be frozen and packed in the camper's chest.

Noah's Ark Chowder

> 2 cans New England style clam chowder
> 2 cans cream of potato soup
> 2 soup cans milk or half-and-half
> 2 tablespoons butter
> Salt, pepper, and chopped parsley, to taste

Combine and simmer in crockpot or any slow cooker 4 hours. Helen Mason, an Arizona cotton wife, came up with this as an easy first course for a patio meal. I'm not convinced Noah's wife did this on the Ark, but it's quick and easy in the camper.

Blushing Bunny

> 1 can tomato soup
> 1 can cheese soup
> 1 cup grated cheese
> 1 egg, optional
> 1 spoonful chili powder
> 1 can water
> 1 can milk

Combine all ingredients, beating together with a fork. Milk may be canned, powdered, or fresh. For a crowd, more water may be added without serious reduction of flavor. Heat, stirring several times, but do not boil. Serve with something crisp — crackers, toast, or pretzels. Serves four to six.

I make a version of this, even quicker, with a can of tomato soup, a can of milk, and a can of chopped green chiles, topped with a sprinkle of white, Mexican, or feta cheese. Some cooks add a can of beer to either soup.

I've never discovered why it's a bunny.

Summer Spa Soup

For the hot and hungry after exercise — mere minutes to make.

> 1 peeled, cubed potato
> 1 chopped onion
> 1/3 cup water
> 1 chicken bouillon cube
> 1 cubed zucchini
> 2 cups buttermilk
> Salt, pepper, and dill to taste

Microwave potato, onion, water, and bouillon (or chicken broth, if available) 2 minutes full power. Add zucchini and cook 2 more minutes. Puree with buttermilk and seasonings. If you don't need a spa soup, use half-and-half. Eat or drink with Pita Wedges. Also delicious chilled.

Pita Wedges. Butter pita bread rounds, cut into eighths, sprinkle with kosher salt, and broil until bubbly. Or sprinkle with cumin and chili powder. Serve hot and make extras. These freeze well for later use.

Arleen's Swedish Fruit Zoop

Our neighbor, Arleen Heminghaus, brought a family inheritance of Swedish recipes from Minnesota to Arizona. This soup is the answer when guests are coming for a patio party and an unexpected chill arrives, too. Warm and comforting, served in mugs, it combines beverage and bulk.

> 1 pound large, pitted prunes
> Cold water
> 1/2 pound seedless raisins
> 1/2 pound currants
> 1 cup brown sugar
> 1/2 cup minute tapioca
> 1 cup wine or grape juice
> Thin lemon slices

In large kettle, generously cover prunes with cold water. Cook 15 minutes. Add raisins and currants. Bring to a simmer and cook an hour, adding water as needed to maintain level 2 inches above fruit. Add brown sugar and tapioca, stirring so tapioca does not ease to bottom in one roe-like lump. When tapioca cooks clear, flavor soup with good grape wine or grape juice. Serve warm, topped with lemon slice. A crispy accompaniment is thin-sliced rye bread, buttered and oven-toasted dry.

(OPPOSITE PAGE) *Two by two, ingredients go together for Noah's Ark Chowder, which works on any houseboat, but also starts meals nicely on the patio or in an RV.*

Time Changes Everything Department

The late Roscoe Willson, then in the U.S. Forest Service, recalled meeting George Hennessey, cattle dealer, in the old Adams Hotel for lunch during a Phoenix heat wave of the 1920s. A newcomer was puzzled when they put their ice on their salads and shook salt into their water.

Willson explained that "old-timers" weren't accustomed to ice in the first place and didn't think it was good practice to put iced water into the stomach when your body was overheated. As to salt, a great deal of body salt was lost through perspiration, so replacement was a must.

Furthermore, there was a time when practically all the water in the Salt River Valley contained noticeable salt. The Salt River flows over salt beds on the Apache Reservation; hence the name. "We got used to it," Willson said. "In fact, we didn't like the taste of water without it. When we got the new water system from the Verde River, it tasted flat. It took a long time to get used to it."

Today, salt tablets are not favored, and salt is not popular with the medical profession. Nevertheless, on the desert trail, we should keep a little shaker handy. Your best buy is sea salt, produced by the evaporation of sea water, rich in minerals. Land-mined rock salt is nothing but sodium chloride and additives, detrimental to health. Salt is essential to human and wildlife. I've never known a cattleman or sheep grower who does not put out and keep a careful eye on salt "licks" to be shared equally by his livestock and wild animals.

Considering the amount of money spent on freeze-dried, packaged camp foods, why not put another dollar into sea salt? Used by the pinch, it lasts for months.

Sangrita-Margarita Legends

How two such simply perfect and perfectly simple libations evolved into egg-white-and-tomato-juice concoctions, I've never discovered. Because both have become a part of Arizona-Sonora lifestyle, especially to those who consider Rocky Point (Puerto Peñasco) and Kino Bay to be second homes, they deserve to be recorded as invented.

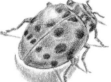

Sangrita
(Widow Sanchez Style)

> 2 ounces orange juice
> 3/4 ounce lemon
>   juice
> 3/4 ounce grenadine
> 1 teaspoon salsa
>   picante
> 1/2 teaspoon
>   Worcestershire Sauce
> 1/2 teaspoon salt
> Cracked ice
> 1 1/2 ounces tequila

Tequila should be chilled. Shake other ingredients to blend with cracked ice. Strain into 6-ounce glass — an unforgettable chaser of orange and chile to follow the natural fire of tequila. The Widow Sanchez invented this throat-closer, eye-opener during the '20s at the Sanchez family restaurant-bar at Lake Chapala, a popular Mexican resort at the time. Most commercial mixes copying this original use tomato juice, Tabasco, and other weak imitations.

(RIGHT) *Sangrita is simple and at its best the way it was invented by the Widow Sanchez at Lake Chapala.*

Margarita

The origin of the Margarita, like the origin of tequila, would make a book, and it has. *The Tequila Book*, by Felipe de Alba and Marion Gorman, explores every anecdote. They say you haven't had a Margarita until you've had one in Mexico — gently, politely shaken (no mixer) together like this.

> Dry salt
> Chipped ice
> 1 1/2 ounces tequila
> 1/2 ounce Triple Sec
> 1 ounce freshly
>   squeezed *limon* juice

Wet rim of chilled cocktail glass with lemon juice then brush with dry salt. Scoop ice into metal shaker, add other ingredients, and gently shake. No gadget to bruise this Margarita. Pour and serve. A *limon* is a Mexican fruit with the best points of its parents, the lemon and the lime. For the American version of the Margarita, check the *Arizona Highways Heritage Cookbook*.

Strawberry Plop Sangria

Sangria was a red wine punch of Spanish origin. In Mexico, it is basically red wine, a sliced orange, lime or lemon, sparkling water, or and a heavy helping of sugar. It is one letter away from Sangrita, but a totally different beverage. No chile, no tequila follow-up in Sangria. But we have added strawberries.

1 **quart large, stemmed, sun-ripened strawberries**
1 **cup sugar**
1 **bottle (fifth) chilled rosé or red wine**
1 **unpeeled seedless orange, sliced**
1 **unpeeled lemon, sliced and seeded**
6 **ounces club soda**
Clear ice cubes
Fresh mint leaves

Marinate strawberries in sugar until heavy syrup develops. Refrigerated overnight works best. To serve, pour into large glass pitcher, reserving a few perfect berries to plop into deep wine or champagne glasses. Add citrus slices to pitcher and stir. Pour soda over fruit and stir again. Fill glasses with ice, then Sangria. Garnish with mint.

Pretty Perks for Quenchers

Beverages for backyard parties, family picnics, tea breaks, or brunches take on more festive appeal with color-bright ice cubes and trims. Let the children or visiting relatives go wild dressing up the drinks. Give them an outside, wipe-off table. It frees you for the big stuff.

Begin with ice. Pick the healthiest specimens — pitted cherries, strawberries, grapes, or fresh fruit squares — to dunk into ice cube trays. Fill with raspberry or lemon-lime sparkling water or ginger ale and freeze. Or freeze cubes of lemonade and iced tea so drinks do not lose flavor as ice melts.

For punch, one big clear plunk of frozen water is better than cubes. If punch is pretty, no need to cloud the bowl with fruity ice. Stainless steel is best for making clear ice. To last, it should be put in the freezer 24 hours in advance. Blocks actually can be made a week in advance, unmolded, wrapped in foil, and stored. To serve, put ice in bottom of bowl, add fresh fruit and hibiscus or other edible flowers that float, then add punch.

Non-alcoholic punch. Squeeze fresh fruit juice just before making punch. I always add one 12-ounce can unsweetened apple juice, unfrozen. It enhances any punch, but subtly. Adding 1 or 2 long slices of cucumber peel imparts fresh, mysterious zest; an English touch. A little bag of juniper berries makes gin-appreciators hopeful. Healthy sparkling waters are better for bubbles than tonic waters, which add quinine.

For sweetening, never add straight sugar. Depending on the kind of punch, use crushed, sweetened fresh fruits, honey, fruit brandies, or make a simple syrup of one part each, water and sugar, boiled until sugar dissolves.

Cool and frosty perks. Dip grape clusters and spears of fresh pineapple or watermelon into a beaten egg white thinned with a little water, then into granulated sugar. Garnish drinks. Dip glasses or thin glass cups with a frosting of lime or lemon sugar.

Make fruit kabobs by threading all kinds of fruits on bamboo skewers or plastic drinking straws. Make kid kabobs for cocoa or chocolate milk with peppermint sticks and marshmallows.

When you scoop out heavy navel oranges or grapefruit to use fruit, save the halves for children's cups. Cut straws in half and float a grape or two. Shells also may be used for baking little coffee cakes or biscuits.

If iced tea clouds, you can clear it once by adding a little boiling water.

Bish's Cappuccino

Bob Bishop dropped into the kitchen one evening when I was pouring coffee for patio guests. He was on vacation from managing several California new-cuisine restaurants. "Cappuccino?" he asked. "No machine," I said. "You don't need a machine," he demonstrated. Like this:

The Mix

**15 teaspoons Ghirardelli
  Chocolate, flaked
2 1/2 shots Tia Maria
Half-and-half to make 1 quart**

Arrange on pretty tray: The Mix, coffee mugs, brandy, and a small bowl of whipped cream. Spoons, of course. Juggle filled tray and hot coffee to courtyard or patio. Assemble.

The Drink

**2 ounces mix in mug
1 ounce brandy
Coffee to fill mug
Float whipped cream atop**

The guests cheered. Helping with the dishes later (this guy is true blue), Bob told me how to whip together a simpler version in camp or RV.

Camp Cappuccino

**3/4 cup warm milk
1 cup strong, black coffee
1 heaped tablespoon dark
  chocolate shavings
Ground cinnamon
Sugar, optional**

Whip or beat warm milk until frothy. In a mug, combine equal amounts of frothy milk and hot coffee. Sprinkle chocolate shavings on top and freckle with cinnamon. Serve with sugar. Yield: 2 cups.

Fresh strawberries frozen inside ice cubes make any patio or picnic sip a more refreshing experience.

Pineapple Bolo

Dick and Caren Seminoff often entertain poolside. Pineapple Bolos are a fruit-and-sip combination guaranteed to put guests into an ease-it attitude.

**1 fresh, ripe
  pineapple per guest
Sugar
Champagne**

Cut top off clean pineapple about 1 1/2 inches from the top. Reserve top. Hollow out pineapple, carefully removing fruit by coring and cutting into sticks. Roll sticks in sugar and replace in shell. Pour champagne into shells to cover sticks. Replace top. Refrigerate Bolos overnight. Serve very chilled from shell. Brandy or rum may be substituted for champagne.

Kahlúa Dreamer

1 quart hot, strong, fresh coffee
1 cup Kahlúa
1/2 cup Napoleon Brandy
4 tablespoons chocolate syrup
2 teaspoons vanilla
6 small scoops ice cream: coffee, vanilla, or light chocolate

If possible, use Mexican Combate coffee or grind fresh coffee beans to make 1 quart coffee. Pour into 6-cup coffee server, not metal. Add Kahlúa, brandy, chocolate syrup, and vanilla. Stir to blend. Pour into warm cups (will hold heat longer) and top each with ice cream of choice. Select favorite Mexican beach to dream about, sip, and tell. Serves three to six.

Hot Buttered Cider

Crockpots normally provide an easy way to slow-cook a wide variety of recipes. "This one," artist Frank King cheerfully remarked, "could get a person potted — or crocked." Frank sometimes took calls at the magazine where I wrote a food column. Once he told an astounded caller to pour the cider down the sink and drink the rum. I hastened to reassure the caller that the recipe is a hot and spicy pleasure just as written, and actually needs no rum at all. She hung up.

1 gallon cider
2 handfuls brown sugar
1 level teaspoon cinnamon
1/4 teaspoon freshly grated nutmeg
1 teaspoon vanilla
2 tablespoons butter
Lemon and orange slices

Combine all ingredients in crockpot and bring to a simmer. Remove lemon and orange slices. If desired, rum can be added, to taste. Alcohol cooks away and only the rum flavor remains. A popular beverage for trick-or-treaters (plain), and easily plugged into an outside circuit.

The Caroler's Wassail Bowl

One of the cheeriest outdoor activities is December caroling, during which the Wassail Bowl is especially appreciated. It warms the hands, clears the throat, and makes standing outside in any weather incredibly pleasant. Dorothy Bentzin-Torbert is the spirit behind this Wassail. Recipes vary from family to family, some adding 1 gallon of cider rather than wine, others adding 2 cups of brandy or rum.

1 cup sugar
4 cinnamon sticks
Lemon slices
2 cups orange juice
2 cups apple juice
7 cups red wine, a burgundy
1/2 cup lemon juice

Boil sugar, cinnamon sticks, and 3 lemon slices in 1/2 cup water 4 or 5 minutes. Strain. Set syrup aside. Combine other ingredients. Heat, but don't boil. Combine with syrup in bowl. Serve hot, with smiles, to 15-20. This is also a good winter camp-out special.

Notes

_____
_____
_____
_____
_____
_____
_____
_____
_____
_____

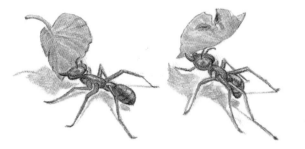

Chapter 11

For the Fun of It

Cooking fun food outdoors has no limits. It's blueberry cobbler in a Dutch oven. It's cooking like the cowboys, forgetting calories and putting gravy on your ranch biscuits. It's going grill crazy and branding everything from pizza dough to hot dogs over the coals. It's sprouting beans or alfalfa on the trail or taking time to stir-fry, maybe steam, wild greens and mushrooms. It's a quick get-together for the kids with backyard ironed pita pockets. It's the surprise of to-each-his-own sandwiches cooked in pie irons. It's the joy of cookies for breakfast (healthy hunks) and mixing your own gorp and, rain or shine, freezing or burning, the exuberant or exhausted pleasure of eating outdoors.

(OPPOSITE PAGE) *If there's a picnic state, it's Arizona. And if there is universal picnic fare, it surely includes hot dogs, hamburgers topped by Bermuda onion rings, sliced tomatoes, sweet or dill pickles, icy lemonade, and watermelon, plus in this case, mandarin orange salad.*

Dutch Oven Magic

Dutch oven cooking is the magic of a hole in the ground, hardwood coals, an iron pot with a tight lid, and a history that goes back to Holland. History says the Pilgrims used this multipurpose pot on the Mayflower where cargo space was scant.

In this stove-oven, we bake biscuits, cobblers and pies, breads and cakes. We also transform wild game into sublime stew. As a soup simmerer and deep-fat fryer, it can't be beat. Dutch oven style enhances chili and emerges from the ashes like Cinderella to parch or pop corn.

Who are "we?" Many of my Dutch oven lessons came from unforgettable Arizona characters who are also writers — Stella Hughes, queen of salty remarks and author of *Chuck Wagon Cookin'*; Bonnie and the late Ed Peplow, whose *Roundup Recipes*, done with the Arizona Cowbelles, is an out-of-print classic worth stealing; Melissa Ruffner and her history-packed papa, Budge Ruffner, who put together the most basic and helpful directions for Dutch oven roasting any novice could hope to find in their *Arizona Territorial Cookbook*. Buy their books and a spider-leg Dutch oven, and you're ready to try the recipes scattered through this outdoor roundup.

Perhaps the most logical mating since Adam and Eve, the hot dog and your favorite chili recipe. Chili Dogs always taste better outdoors.

Frankly Best

The National Hot Dog and Sausage Council says we consume seven hot dogs per person every month. That adds up to 50 million a day. From tailgate meals to stick cooking, frankly speaking, nothing beats 'em for speed and choice of fixin's. Whether they are based on beef, pork, turkey, or chicken, balance their fat and nitrates with the vitamin C in green salads and fresh fruits.

Dog Kabobs. Cut each frank into 4 pieces. Alternate on skewer with pineapple chunks and sweet pepper squares. Brush with salad oil. Broil over hot coals (tap coals or briquets lightly if covered with gray ash), turning until browned.

Bean Dogs. *Boston style*: Split wieners lengthwise, spread with sweet pickle relish, fill with Boston baked beans. Wrap each in double thickness of heavy foil. Grill 5 minutes on coals, turning once. Toast rolls as dogs cool enough to unwrap. *Southwest style*: Split wieners but fill with chili beans and proceed. *Arizona style*: Split dogs and fill with incendiary chili, no beans.

Goober Dogs. Split franks lengthwise and spread with peanut butter. Wrap in lean bacon strip. Do a half-dozen at a time in grill basket over coals, turning once. Slide into toasted rolls.

Burrito Burgers

It takes time for Easterners who move to Arizona to accept the speckled pinto bean and its mashed version, the refry. Kids take to refried beans after one warm, tasty, somewhat squishy bean burro (seasoned beans wrapped inside a flour tortilla). This is a wonderful way to stretch a pound of ground beef.

1 pound ground beef
2 tablespoons chopped chiles from 4-ounce can
1/4 cup finely chopped onion
1/2 teaspoon salt
1 cup refried beans
4 thin slices cheese
8 flour tortillas
1 cup chopped lettuce or cabbage
1 cup chopped tomato

Combine beef, chiles, onion, and salt. Mix with hands. Add beans and mix well. Form 8 patties. Cut cheese slices in half and put on one side of patty. Press edges to seal cheese. Grill over medium coals about 5 minutes per side. Heat tortillas, 6- or 8-inch size, on side of grill. Center burgers on tortillas, top with lettuce, tomato, and remaining green chiles. Wrap and eat. Burrito Burgers can be made and frozen to take on hikes or picnics.

Pie Irons

Mary Riemersma began food packing for an extended weekend of camping after breakfast at 8. The family left Phoenix at 9, knowing they'd be chowing down happily every day on pie-iron breakfast, pie-iron pepperoni pizza, and pie-iron grilled cheese sandwiches. Mary also had frozen crepes and meatballs. "Who needs to fill the chest with ice when you can pack it with freezer bundles for meals?" she asks.

Mary used to be stuck with an array of cooking pans and the associated cleanup until she discovered pie irons and the Dutch oven. Pie irons, available at most camp stores and K-Mart, are circles of metal on two long handles.

"Virtually anything can be cooked in pie irons," Mary says. "They are a great opportunity for kids to be creative. You can use them over any fire, even a fireplace. The condition of the coals is not a primary concern, as the cooker determines how closely the iron is held to the heat. There are few utensils to wash; just each person's iron. With a green salad, pie-iron pizza provides a well-balanced meal." For pizza, use good, dense bread, not thickly sliced; add tomato sauce, cheese, and other toppings.

For breakfast, lightly butter the outside of two bread slices, or spray the pie iron with oil or Pam. Center an egg on one slice and top with cheese or a slice of ham. Put on the other bread slice, clamp shut, cook over an open fire, and enjoy!

The best way to turn out a sandwich over any fire — the handy pie iron (shown here with the lid removed).

Backyard Ironed Pita Pockets

When I was a Cub Scout den co-mother, the pack thought its funniest cooking lesson was ironing melted cheese sandwiches between sheets of foil. Quickest, too. We had three outdoor outlets and a big picnic table; they took turns ironing. Hand everybody at least two 12-inch pieces of heavy-duty foil, two slices of sturdy bread or pita bread cut to make a pocket, and let them build a filling.

Fillings:
Thin dry salami and Swiss cheese

Pork barbecue and little pineapple chunks

Monterey jack cheese, tomato slices, and diced chiles

Fajita chicken chunks and grated cheese

Sliced hot dogs, sauerkraut, and diced apples

Butter bread or pita lightly on both sides after filling. Wrap in foil. Set hot iron on top long enough to melt cheese and heat sandwich through — about 1 minute.

Wise Barbecue for 75

This barbecue on buns was fun for the kids at Shadow Valley Ranch in Prescott, and for the seniors at Abiding Savior Lutheran Church, who loved to take it along on picnics. And it's fun for the cook, who can turn it out in a hurry.

Anabel Wise, a sky-blue-eyed Norwegian who cooks, indoors or out, for crowds of up to 300, says: "This is such a simple recipe. I recommend it for any group, remembering to adjust the chili powder to the taste of the eater."

16 pounds fresh, lean ground beef
5 cans (12-ounce) tomato sauce
2 large bottles (14-ounce) catsup
1/4 can or jar chili powder, for starters

In several huge skillets or Dutch ovens, brown meat. Drain off all fat. Add other ingredients. Depending on the crowd, Anabel uses up to a whole can of chili powder, any available brand, but the fresher the better. Add by taste. Simmer until barbecue is well-blended. Serve on plain buns. Halve or double recipe as needed.

T.J.'s Sinful Treats

Some people have to improve perfection. Homemade granola is really nutritious. T.J., a friend, came up with this way to disguise granola in a bar cookie.

Boil 2 minutes: 1 cup brown sugar mixed with 1/2 cup corn-oil. Pour over cookie sheet lined with graham crackers, generously sprinkled with granola and extra raisins. Bake 10 minutes at 350 degrees. Reasonably healthy; unreasonably tempting.

Cookies for Breakfast

The John Schwadas moved to Tempe in 1971 when he became president of Arizona State University. His wife, Wilma, found that Cookies for Breakfast got four Schwadas off to a quick, healthy start. A welcome change from bacon and eggs, they are also ideal for camping, hiking, and lunch bags.

1 cup soft butter or margarine
1 cup firmly packed brown sugar
1 cup granulated sugar
2 large eggs
1 teaspoon vanilla
2 cups flour, all-purpose or whole grain
1 teaspoon each, baking powder and soda
1/2 teaspoon salt
2 cups regular or quick rolled oats
1 cup Grape-nuts
1 cup pitted, chopped dates
1 cup shredded coconut

In the large bowl of an electric mixer, beat together butter and sugars until creamy. Beat in eggs, one at a time. Add vanilla. Mix together flour, baking powder, soda, salt, rolled oats in another bowl. Add Grape-nuts, dates, and coconut. When well-blended, stir into creamed mixture. Hands may be needed; mixture is very stiff and may halt mixer. Drop by level tablespoon onto greased cookie sheets, placing dough 2 inches apart. Bake in preheated, 375-degree oven 10 minutes or until golden brown. Makes 7 dozen cookies. Or 3 dozen breakfasts!

The Gravy Boat

As the family grew, Shirley Young of Phoenix found hamburger was her staple. "I'll bet Bill's favorite meal is SOS," she says. "Just brown a pound of hamburger and take off any fat. Add 4 tablespoons of flour and 2 cups of fresh or canned milk to make a gravy. Salt and pepper it and serve over biscuits or toast." This is today's version of the pioneer's jerky gravy. It's still the quick, hearty way to feed husbands, Scouts, campers, and hunters.

SOS is not to be confused with another gravy dear to the southern spirit — Red Eye — perfect for camping or RV trips. Sue Mitchell Claxton, who served many major dinners for Governor John C. Phillips in 1928, told me how to make *real* Red Eye Gravy.

"Fry a thick slice of good country ham until nice and brown. Remove the ham and drain off excess fat, but leave browned drippings in the skillet. Pour fresh coffee from the pot into the pan and bring the gravy to a boil, stirring. (If you use milk, it gets thicker and it isn't Red Eye.) Serve with ham and homemade biscuits. Eggs, too, if you want." I want.

J & J Gorp

" . . . and I need some gorp," said my high-school-age son, Scott, as he packed for his first hike into the Grand Canyon. Gorp? My food-writing files bulged with foreign recipes — but gorp?

Joyce and Jean Rukkila, neighboring twins and sisterly mentors, solemnly gave us the recipe which, with granola, accounts for the sound of teeth grinding through the wilderness all over the world. Mix as desired and seal in plastic baggies:

◆ Sunflower and pumpkin seeds, salted peanuts, apple and banana chips, M & Ms (they don't melt like chips), raisins, and pretzel sticks. That's for starters.

Since then, I've discovered that some trail-munchers add dry milk to keep things from sticking and to beef up the protein. The excuse for this glorious jumble of fun food is to reinforce energy. In the wilds, you actually need carbohydrates and salt to keep your body fueled and fortified.

Fellow food writer Pat Myers kept her family of four moving with a gorp that included gum, sourballs, Tootsie Rolls, jerky, cocktail pretzels, and cheese.

Some trail cooks pour the nuts and seeds and chips onto a cookie sheet, drizzle butterscotch and chocolate chips over all, then cut the result into chunks for wrapping. Others spice seeds and nuts with a little soy sauce and chili powder. To each his own taste. Do not overload on these energizers, and do sit down to snack.

(LEFT) Gorp contains whatever the gorp-maker declares that it should. In this case, black-eyed Susans peek around a mix that includes peanuts, pumpkin seeds, and shelled sunflower seeds.

Sprout Sense

Sprouting makes special sense when you're somewhere in the "boonies" and salads or wild greens are scarce. In fact, Owen Baynham, Colorado River runner, sprouted on the white waters for a decade. "Quick and crisp on sandwiches and great in omelets," he enthuses.

Buy untreated seeds. Alfalfa and mung beans are easily sprouted — like this:

In the evening, put about 2 tablespoons seeds or beans in a quart jar and cover with water. You must have a lid with holes or nylon net or cheesecloth to secure this glass garden. In the morning, with lid in place, pour off water. Add fresh, warmish, not hot, water and slosh to rinse seeds. Pour off and add cool water, then pour off and put jar in cool, dark place in your pack, camper, or bike bag. When you stop for a drink, give your seeds a drink.

Don't be surprised when beans double in bulk, giving you twice the B vitamins and iron. Rinse 3 times a day and always keep the jar on its side, tilted enough that seeds don't lie in water. Within two days, sprouts are edible. Rinse and share. They don't keep more than a day in hot weather. Sugar and protein for pennies.

Happy Valley Hot Flash

For retirees Norm and Flo Fickeisen, life is a gardening picnic on a 10-acre desert hillside near Carefree. Norm takes his daily garden-to-greenhouse-to-orchard tour, and picks. It's up to Flo to transform the pickings. "This goes with fish, game, eggs — a Hot Flash of vitamins," she promises. Equal parts Flash and sour cream make a dynamite dip.

> 1 quart cherry tomatoes
> 2 medium jalapeño
>   peppers, fresh
> 1 medium onion, cut up
> 1 medium bell pepper,
>   cut and seeded
> 2 garlic cloves
> 1/2 cup herb vinegar
> 1 teaspoon each,
>   sugar and salt
> Oregano, dried and crushed
> Cayenne and ground cumin

In blender, coarsely grind tomatoes. Add other vegetables and blend. Transfer to small stainless steel pot. Add vinegar, salt, and sugar. Simmer, uncovered, to desired consistency, stirring in herbs to taste. Yield, 4 pints.

N o t e s

_____

_____

_____

_____

_____

_____

_____

_____

_____

_____

CHAPTER 12

While You Wait

You're waiting and you're starving. What can you do and eat that will not ruin your appetite for the grilled rosemary chicken, the mesquite-broiled steaks, the foiled fish and veggies.

This is the time to bring equal rights into the picture. Divide the group into fuel gatherers, water buddies, cooking companions, and, for those who like to put things off, cleanup candidates.

Campers find this a good time to teach children or novices the value of searching out fire materials (where wood fires are allowed) with no damage to the environment. Then how to build a safe fire, close to food preparation but away from grass or combustibles. Kids can assume duties as fire watchers and man water pistols as flare dousers.

Whether at the pool or on the patio — on a float adventure or under the pines — quick, light snacks soothe impatient tummies. Ideally, you fix fruit and vegetable finger food, and a healthy dip. A crockpot of dunk or peppered popcorn, quick lemonade or a chilled beer, quell the hunger, quench the thirst, and ease the pressure. Enjoy the charm of improvised eating. You've felt the pleasure of body movement — now it's easy time — and food is the focus.

(OPPOSITE PAGE) *An antipasto tray welcomes Lake Powell houseboaters while the main course is cooking. Most houseboats have outside grills, providing the best of all Arizona worlds — sunny days, starry nights, clean air, emerald water, lovely scenery, and of course, delectable food.*

The Incredible Bean Ball

"Instant" or precooked beans are an ancient form of traveling food, according to Carolyn Niethammer, author of *Tumbleweed Gourmet*. Her camping bean recipe calls for tepary beans, so important to the Tohono O'odham Indian tribe of Arizona. Their creation myth recounts how the Milky Way was formed out of the small white tepary.

Tepary beans are hard to find, but pinto or pink beans, while not as nutritious, are sold almost everywhere and taste yummy, as refried bean lovers know.

2 cups teparies or pinto beans
2 garlic cloves, chopped or minced
1 onion, chopped
Salt and pepper to taste

Clean beans and soak overnight. Some backpackers soak beans in plastic bags hanging from their packs by day. (Teparies need plenty of soaking time.) Drain, rinse, and cook in water to cover with garlic and onion, lid on. When soft, mash some of the beans against the kettle with the back of a spoon, and stir into beans to make a thick, rich broth. Stir often, keeping heat low. (Beans burn if you turn your back on them.) Season to taste. Spread on a heavy cookie sheet and allow to dry so thoroughly they can be broken into chunks and stored in plastic bags. For easy use when backpacking or camping, add water, heat, and eat. Makes 2 cups.

Carl Franz, in his *On-Off-the-Road Cookbook*, refines this recipe to make a miracle bean ball that he says will keep an amazing length of time. However, he jazzes up the beans as they cook with a tablespoon each of oil, cumin, oregano, and chili powder. He uses garlic powder because he thinks fresh garlic won't keep as long after being cooked into the beans.

He refries the beans until they are very thick and dry. When they've cooled enough to handle, mold them into a ball or a cake. Once cold, wrap in a clean cloth or brown paper. He believes plastic bags trap moisture and encourage spoilage. Eat the bean ball cold with bread, a tortilla, or fresh vegetable, or fry it with onion, tomatoes, and cheese. Dissolved, it's good soup. In cool weather, it keeps up to four days. Incredible.

Camp Quickies, REI Style

Sue Cullumber, REI outreach supervisor, has some quick-fry tricks to appease camp helpers as they fix the fire, find water, and make shelter for the night.

Cheesy Biscuits. Use biscuit mix, your own or commercial, but add garlic and pepper. Make up and put a bit of cheese inside each spoonful of mixture. Drop into small amount of oil over fire. When golden brown, cheese should be melted. Instant disappearing acts.

Stir Fries. Instead of cheese, put small pieces of veggies, even if slightly wilted, inside the dough.

Backpacker's Pizza. Add water to bread mix or biscuit dough and flatten into patties. Fry until golden. Top with tomato sauce, cheese, freeze-dried veggies, green peppers, or mushrooms. All or a few may be used.

Brenna's Chile con Queso Dunk

Joyce Brooks cooks for groups of from four to 50, using daughter Brenna's slightly chunky dunk for an appetizer. She scatters crockpots out on her porch near outlets. This dunk is best served hot.

- **1 can cheddar cheese soup**
- **1 can stewed tomatoes with juice**
- **1 4-ounce can chopped green chiles**
- **1 small onion, chopped**
- **1 bunch green onions, diced with tops**

Mix in the crockpot and stir. Heat about 1 hour. Serve with baskets of fresh corn chips for dunking. Serves 20. It may be made hotter with a larger can of chiles.

Dunk works just as well on a houseboat, or in the RV circle — in short, anywhere there is an electrical outlet.

(LEFT AND ABOVE) When the nearest pizza parlor is in the world you left behind in order to hit the trail, Backpacker's Pizza responds to your craving. (Recipe on opposite page.)

Diane's Vegetable Squares

Diane Nasser has this answer to keeping appetites under control during dip-and-drip time around the pool. Heaped with vegetables, one recipe yields 50-60 squares.

8 ounces cream cheese
1 cup mayonnaise
1 package powdered ranch dressing
1 cup each, grated carrots,
broccoli, cauliflower
1 package crescent rolls

Remove crescents from package and spread across a rectangular cookie sheet, pressing all seams together. Bake (inside or on outdoor grill) according to package directions and let cool. Have ready cream cheese, mayonnaise, and ranch dressing, mixed together until smooth. Spread over baked crust. Sprinkle generously with grated vegetables. Cut into small squares. Impossible to eat merely one.

Skillet Navajo Taco

Irene Kline used to make a skillet pizza over the campfire. Then she came to Arizona and became involved in directing a cookbook for the prestigious Heard Museum. Now she makes a Navajo Taco skillet-style, as a quick first course.

A greased iron or nonstick skillet
Bisquick dough to fill bottom of skillet
Chile-tomato sauce
Toppings of beans and crumbled beef
Shredded cheese

The skillet must have a tight lid. Cook over medium coals until dough is cooked, bottom is browned, and cheese melted. It can be done with Pillsbury refrigerated dough, too. And the recipe for Dried Ground Beef Mix (page 152) is a natural topper. Slice in wedges and serve with real or nonalcoholic Bloody Marys. Filled skillet serves four to six.

Outreach Stew

This all-Arizona blend of flavor is the kitchen brainstorm of Daniel Scharf, coordinator of Southwest Regional Outreach Services. It combines tasty ingredients from many areas. Cook and freeze to take camping, Arizona style.

3 pounds lean beef
(from feedlots of Stanfield)
1 medium onion, diced
(from Yuma)
2 medium carrots, peeled and chopped
(from Avra Valley)
1 cup lima beans, precooked
(from Willcox)
2 medium roasted sweet corn, shucked
(from Elfrida)
1/4 head cabbage, chopped
(from Gila Bend)
8 large snow peas, blanched, cut bite size
(from Flagstaff)
3 ounces mild green chile peppers, diced
(from Sasabe)
4 ounces red wine
(from Webb Winery, Tucson)
2 tablespoons flour as thickener
(from Hayden Mill, Tempe)
1 teaspoon salt
(from open mine, Glendale)

The beef should be browned in nonstick pan and corn should be sliced off ears. Then vegetables, meat, and salt can be put in slow cooker with 1/2 cup Arizona Crystal water. Simmer for the day. When vegetables and meat are tender, add wine and thicken with flour. Serve with Indian fry bread made in Keams Canyon. Serves six. This recipe was a gift to the Friends of Rehab at Good Samaritan Hospital, Phoenix, for their fund-raising cookbook.

Black Bean & Pepper Pleasure

This is bean salad with a difference. The jalapeño adds a touch of fire for those who like it. Nutritionally, this combination is sound since the vitamin C in the peppers and tomato doubles the amount of iron you absorb from the beans.

> 1 16-ounce can black beans,
>   rinsed and drained
> 1 large green bell pepper, seeded and diced
> 1/2 cup tomato, seeded and diced
> 2 scallions, thinly sliced
> 1 jalapeño pepper, seeded
>   and minced (optional)
> 2 teaspoons olive or vegetable oil
> 4 teaspoons lemon juice
> 1/8 teaspoon each, pepper,
>   freshly ground, and sea salt

Toss all vegetables well in a medium bowl. In a small bowl or jar, combine oil, juice, and jalapeño pepper until well blended. Pour dressing over bean mixture and toss well to coat. It's healthy. Nutritionist Francie Mallery says the jalapeño makes it perfect . . . try it! But wear rubber gloves while working with jalapeños, always. From *An Ounce of Prevention*, an American Institute for Cancer Research cookbook.

Historic Nutty Nibbles

Piñons. You are indulging in historic food. Pine nuts were found in the ruins of Pompeii and in Arizona's ancient pueblos. Piñons grow in Italy (the prized *pignolia*), Spain, Taiwan, and, in two-inch-seed form, in South America. The piñon, a gnarled evergreen tree, has grown for millennia in Arizona.

Its small, oval nuts, recorded by explorers as far back as Cabeza de Vaca, were gathered for food and trade, and still are. If you think the little bags of piñon nuts are expensive at specialty stores and trading posts, remember the climbing, shaking, and sorting that garnered them.

Some old recipes are still in use. The sweet, delicate nutmeat is ground to use with other flour or to enrich a stew. Desert Indians mix them with yucca fruits which have been baked on coals. Mexican cooks use them in candy and bread puddings. After harvest, the Hopis met with grandmother around a bowl of freshly roasted Tuva (piñon nuts) to hear clan history, wrote Juanita Tiger Kavena.

Their method: Clean nuts and wash in clear water several times, then roast in pan about 20 minutes, stirring to prevent burning. Make a salt brine of 1 tablespoon salt to 1 cup water and sprinkle lightly over hot nuts. Return to oven to dry. After they cool, a gifted piñon eater can crack the steely shells in his mouth, retain the nutmeat as he expels the fragments, and enjoy rare crunching.

Paria Nachos

Lee Michlipsy teaches "Know Your Resources" workshops for the cities of Mesa and Phoenix. As her students become familiar with the Sonoran life zone, they also pick up camp cooking. While waiting for Dutch oven food to cook tender, they cheer the news that they'll be forced to eat calories to keep the energy flowing. "Paria Nachos (named for beautiful Paria Canyon in northern Arizona) are wildly popular with instant lemonade," Lee finds. "Or a margarita, if we're settled for the overnight."

**12 small corn tortillas,
uncooked
2 tablespoons vegetable oil
1/2 cup grated jalapeño cheese
1/4 cup grated longhorn cheese**

Cut tortillas into quarters. In a large skillet (nonstick is least hassle), sauté chips over moderate heat in light oil. When they begin to crisp, remove from heat and sprinkle with cheeses. Devour when cheeses melt. Serves four. Great to accompany a meal of chili, too.

(OPPOSITE PAGE) *Paria Nachos are a quick, hot snack flavored by corn chips, cheeses, and jalapeños, guaranteed to stave off hunger pangs during the pre-dinner waiting period.*

A Prospector's Picnic

The lure of silver took John Berry, a young mining engineer, into the desert foothills with a burro and two Mexican miners. A cooking fire devastated their camp, and they faced a 24-hour hike without food or water.

"Don't worry, I'll find both for us," one of the miners said. When he sighted a mescal plant sending up its tender shoot, he cut and peeled the 2-foot shoot and divided it. It was full of juice and tasted a little like jicama or raw potato. Through the long walk, they refreshed themselves as they found mescal. (Remember, *not* barrel cactus juice!)

At sunup, they came upon a goat ranch where coffee and tortillas were cooking on a sheet of iron. The ranch owner not only shared his breakfast, he dug into his fire with a shovel and brought up something steaming in a burlap sack. It was a cow's head which had been baking underground 3 days. With knives, they dug out the meat, wrapped it in flour tortillas, and pronounced it one of the best breakfasts ever. And an outdoor meal to remember.

Seedy Energizers

Chia Seeds. The minuscule, black chia seed is the mighty mite of the desert, gathered from a type of wild sage and almost weightless. Indians made use of them as sustenance on long desert treks to gather salt.

Ted De Grazia, famed Arizona artist, told me he lived on chia seeds and water for five days while retracing one of Fray Marcos de Niza's journeys, to authenticate a book he was writing. "They're full of protein and energy. Besides," he grinned, "they invade every space between your teeth and turn into a chewy jelly. You can cover miles while your tongue tries to dislodge them for eating. De Niza always had a little pouch of chia seeds." Chia seeds are so mucilaginous they cannot be sprouted like most seeds but, for some reason, do well in those little Mexican earthenware animals made for the purpose. It's best to take a pouch like the friars and De Grazia. Chia seeds are available in health food stores.

Pumpkin Seeds *(Pepitas)*. Save the seeds when you carve a jack-o'-lantern or make a pumpkin pie or cake. I scatter mine on a Teflon cookie tray to dry in the oven with a little olive oil, salt, and butter. They add crunch and zesty flavor to salads, snacks, and rice.

You can also fry them on the grill in a heavy iron skillet with a teaspoon of peanut oil and a drift of salt or chili powder. I like chewing the whole seed; most people prefer the inner kernel, sold as *pepitas*. Often they are oversalted, but this can be an advantage when perspiration removes body salts.

A favorite nibble is made even better when popcorn is popped over an open fire.

Dried Ground Beef Mix

Nothing cheers a river- or trail-tired, half-starved outdoorsman (or woman) more than the announcement that dinner will take only five minutes. It's no spoof when you dry your own meat for tacos or mix meals.

    1 pound lean ground beef or lamb
    2 garlic cloves
    1/2 cup finely chopped onion
    1 tablespoon Tamari
      (natural soy sauce)
    2 tablespoons flour or masa
    1/2 teaspoon each, salt and pepper

Smash and dice garlic. Brown beef with garlic and onion, draining off every drop of fat. It's important to have lean meat and drain all fat. Add remaining ingredients and cook over medium heat, stirring so mix browns evenly. Spread on Pam-sprayed or lightly oiled cookie sheet. Dry in 140-degree oven about 6 hours. Prop door slightly open. Allow to cool and pack for camp or freezer. To reconstitute, add 1 3/4 cups water. Simmer 5 minutes. Feeds three hungry hikers when combined with rice, pasta, or instant potatoes. Mix with beans for quick chili, or stir into spaghetti sauce.

First American Nibbles

Popcorn. Although popcorn is thought to have originated in Mexico from wild grass, native Americans civilized it by mixing kernels of sweet corn vigorously with hot sand in a clay pot. Light enough to carry hiking, low in calories (as is), and quickly popped, it is an ideal wait watcher and pacifier. If you're ravenous, toss some salted peanuts into the bowl. If you're adventurous, try some of these:

Crazy, Mixed-Up Popcorn. To unbuttered popcorn, add: granola; chopped, dried fruit; raisins; crumbled crisp bacon; crumbled French-fried onions or potatoes; sunflower or pumpkin seeds; any kind of nut; chocolate, peanut butter, or butterscotch bits. It's best to stop with one or two additions, although for a patio party you could challenge the children to come up with the tastiest mix.

Topped-out Popcorn. Add Parmesan cheese with a little dry salad dressing mix, or wheat or oat germ, with seeds; curry or chili powder; honey, maple, or blueberry syrup. All cling better if popcorn is hot and buttered before toppings are drizzled on, then tossed.

Raisin-Pecan Popcorn. To unbuttered popcorn, add 1 cup Arizona pecan pieces, 1/2 cup Arizona pistachios, and 1 cup raisins. Then toss with a syrup made by mixing 1/4 cup melted butter with 1 heaping tablespoon pumpkin pie spice. Pistachios are optional and expensive, but worth it.

Peanuts and Sunflower Seeds. Arizona has been producing peanuts since the 1930s, and sunflower seeds since the days when Indians ate root, stalk, and seed. Eaten together, they are powerhouse protein.

A Note to the Spirits

Outdoor meals are becoming more and more spirited. As I researched recipes for this book, I was surprised at the number of dishes that are cooked with wine, beer, or spirits of some sort.

In marinades, over desserts, as a part of ice creams and coffees, on fish, to tame game, even in chili con carne, a splash of Chablis or a quarter-cup of 80-proof cognac seem to be taking the place of water or stock.

My chapter on *Quenchers* contains cautious reference to spirits because spirits usually do *not* quench thirst. Most outdoor cookbooks are indexed thus: "Alcohol, see Fuel." Most outdoor cookbook authors consider alcoholic beverages a luxury, yet many campers consider them a staple — the evening hours after a hot hike or river run are more pleasant with a cold beer.

Spiked cooking is with us to stay. A few rules from the experts guide us through. When poaching, simmer wine 15 to 20 minutes before adding fish or chicken, thus giving the alcohol time to cook away bitterness, mellowing flavor. To flambé spirits without the danger of flare-up, heat in pan with a long handle and avert your face as you ignite the dish. Beer foams up in cooking, as it does when poured into a glass. Add slowly.

Notes

_____

_____

_____

_____

_____

_____

_____

_____

Chapter 13

S'mores

The simple, unsung sweetheart of outdoor cookery is known as S'mores — or "some mores" — that satisfying mix of toasted marshmallow, melted chocolate, and crisp graham cracker that puts the time-honored finishing touch on a fresh-air meal.

This chapter rounds up S'mores of a different sort: some more campfire tips, some more campsite hints, some more cooking and grilling helps, and still more shopping and packing suggestions.

Put 'em together and use them to ensure a less-hassled, more satisfying experience. They add up to smart, low-impact cooking. It isn't intimidating when you use the how-tos given freely by experts in grass-roots gourmet and environmental good housekeeping.

Best time to start is before you cook. If ever menu planning is a must, it is prior to outdoor chef-ing. Simply put, much done ahead means less to do in camp, on the patio, at a picnic, on the boat, or *apres-ski*.

Cooking in the backyard and cooking in camp may vary a lot, but one rule prevails: "The food is the fun."

One friend, a constant griller, summed it up: "When we have people over for barbecue, we never tell them the steaks or fish will be ready when they come. Involve the guests. The idea is: This is casual; wear your shorts, and the entertainment is *cooking*!" That's even more true on the trail.

(OPPOSITE PAGE) *Camping and fishing, with some time out for hiking the back trails, is the ultimate outdoor experience for many. Outdoor cooking, when carefully planned and lovingly executed, can be the "extra" that makes a good time perfect. This Arizona couple, camping along the Black River, studied tips and checklists in advance — leaving themselves nothing to do but have fun.*

◆ On The Trail ◆

*Simple and lightweight, keeping weight to a minimum, 35 mm film canisters
(carefully labeled) tote many ingredients and tuck easily into backpacks.*

Stove
Biodegradable soap
Fuel
Plastic pot scrubber
Grate
Paper dish towels
Heavy foil
35-mm film canisters for spices, herbs, cooking oil
Canteen or water bottles
Reclosable bags
Crush-proof folding cup
Whistle
Nesting cook set
Wide-mouth thermos, pint
Lexan cutlery set
Trash bags
Food squeeze tubes
Pot grabber
Can-bottle opener
Butane lighters or matches
Water purifying pills

Backpackers' Delights

If speed is the cooking criterion, backpack gourmet may be your choice. Eating on the trail has changed dramatically since Arizona's early mountain men considered a full pack to be one pound of salt and five pounds of cornmeal. The mountain was their market and their source of fuel.

A backpack stove in a stuff sack would have brought a snicker from old Bill Williams — as would have Enchantment Granola (recipe on page 24). Hikers, climbers, river runners, bikers, and campers have an ever-enlarging choice of equipment. Nevertheless, use the backpacker's rule: "Keep it simple and light."

Where and how you are going determines what you take. Rules are set. Take them into account. Arizona has six national forests totaling more than 11 million acres. Camping and hiking are permitted anywhere not posted or fenced off. No motorized travel in wilderness areas. Respect the land, other campers, and wildlife. Pack out all trash. Put out all fires — completely. The same rules apply in state park campgrounds.

Stringent rules are in the wings. Outdoor camp cooking in the forests, as practiced for generations, must change. The primal fascinations with fire, blazing a trail, chopping wood, stripping saplings for cooking sticks, etc., are no longer suitable.

Why not? Cliff Blake, a national coordinator for the U.S. Forest Service , explains: "There were about 18 million visitors to the national forests in 1946. Now we are looking at 225 million a year."

In the early 1980s, the Forest Service vigorously began promoting "no trace" camping. Hoping to guide the next generation, they urged Boy and Girl Scouts and Campfire Boys and Girls to become environmentally aware campers. The latest Boy Scout Manual is written accordingly. "Bury your hatchets; forget fire rings; cook on a small portable stove, not coals." We must camp with an eye to preservation.

Trailwise backpackers may settle for foods that don't require cooking, or they may cook a lot at home to freeze or package as meals to be heated up in camp. There are also easily prepared dry meals — powdered drinks and soups, pastas, rice and lentils, cereals and mixes — add water and backpackers keep trudging.

First night out for many means steak and wine as gourmets on the trail practice culinary one-upmanship. This book has its upscale recipes, but it settles for a practical, almost bare bones equipment list for cooking.

It's dinner in the back country for this backpacker, camping along Campaign Creek in the Tonto National Forest.

Camping on Wheels

The first Conestoga wagon was put together in Pennsylvania for pioneers who were planning to move about freely. They were advised to equip it with Dutch ovens and skillets, tin cups and plates, a water keg, two churns (one for sweet milk, one for sour), and a sheet-iron stove.

The chuck wagon, of necessity, dropped the churns (no milk cows) and added the sourdough keg and a chuck box for coffee, beans, spices, sugar, lard, rice, dried fruit, and molasses. From Conestoga wagon to chuck wagon to today's RVs, Americans have hit the road, cooking all the way.

More than 30 million Americans own or rent those homes on wheels, or RVs. Some spend their lives moving about. As with all campers, they find the air smells purer, the food tastes better, and the kitchen can be inside or out.

Much of the equipment and many of the tools listed in this chapter come with RV territory, too. Kitchen musts are kept to a minimum and shopped for with care because they will last a generation.

Picnics, Portable Meals & Movable Feasts

"Picnic" appeared in our language about 1748, the American shortcut for the French word *piquenique*, which translated into "a fashionable social entertainment with each party present contributing a share of the provisions."

My husband once said, "Pick up whatever food we've got, and let's get the nick out of here." Coming to Phoenix in the 1940s, we settled into a pattern of summer picnics in Phoenix's shady, lagoon-cooled Encanto Park, and winter picnics in cactus-studded South Mountain Park. Picnic possibilities today beckon ice-chest crowds to table sites, provided in growing numbers throughout this wondrous state.

Equipment for picnics at home or roadside is basically the same. The trick is having the basics in one place. Always return these items to the basket or tote bag after a picnic. Many an outing has been cut short for lack of an opener or foil. Make a checklist that works for *your* picnics.

◆ Picnickers Checklist ◆

For Food
Lidded basket or big tote
Ice chest or coolers
Table or ground cover
Plates, cups, flatware
Can, bottle, and wine openers
Knife with protective cover
Thermoses
Paper towels
Heavy foil
Plastic bags
Containers with tight lids

For Safety
First aid kit
Flashlight
Bug repellent
Extra water jugs, filled
Small shovel
Butane lighter or matches
Biodegradable liquid soap

(OPPOSITE PAGE) *The RV takes bed and breakfast (plus lunch, dinner, and more) to Hart Prairie, where fall colors paint the San Francisco Peaks. Most RVers are basically camp cooks, but if the weather is less than ideal, they step inside to the built-in LP gas range.*

Packing It Up

A backpacking trip can be snafued by thoughtless placing of gear and food in the pack. Cooking gear should go on the bottom of the large, upper section of the backpack. Food should be protected from soaps and liquid fuels. Seal everything tightly. Color-code stuff sacks for lunch, dinner, snacks. Outside pockets are best for the gorp, apples, or things most often reached for. Heavy foil can wrap, cook, or serve as a makeshift cup or pan, as well as a windscreen and heat reflector. Use the foil over and over, and pack it out, along with plastic bags. Hungry animals following the smell of food have choked to death on such temptations.

Use 35-mm film cartridges to carry such necessities as salt, chili pepper, sugar, cocoa, dry milk, and herbs — *and label them!* Or use reclosable bags. Mix dry ingredients to rehydrate later — and wet ingredients, too — in sturdy, reclosable bags, and that's one less bowl to clean later.

Sort items by meals — a bag or box of breakfast items, then lunch, dinner, and snacks, with the needed foil, paper towels, and utensils. A lightweight, sturdy packing aid is an empty cardboard six-pack carton, which makes a handy holder for rolls of foil, paper towels, plastic wrap, a small bottle of biodegradable soap, and a shaker of baking soda.

Soda puts out small fires, combines with water as an antacid, takes pine pitch off your hands, makes a cooling powder for feet and shoes, and sweetens the holding tank in your RV.

Everyone who travels with liquid fuels should have a fuel flask with a spout-lid combination that doesn't leak when closed. And *never* carry food and fuel in the same pack. Nor should soaps, insect sprays, and toiletries be placed with foods. A good soap trick is a net bag filled with all those little leftover soap pieces we used to throw away. No more soap slipping onto the pine needles. Remember, a little dab of lather will do ya' — there's a whole new water game out there. Soap (even biodegradable) is an additional load on environmental decomposers.

Picnic supplies should be packed in the reverse order of use: Food on the bottom, serving pieces next, tablecloth across the top with flat cakes and breads underneath, positioned next to the paper towels and napkins. Ice chests work best with a layer of ice on the bottom. Drinks, salads, and fruits ride the ice, and salad greens top out in a plastic bag. At serving time, toss greens with dressing in the same bag.

Finally, do not be intimidated by the overabundance of cooking machines, fuels, and gadgets. Remember the rule: If all else fails, read the instructions. Whether trail trekking or poolside partying, boatnicking, or tailgating, the whole idea is to snatch every chance to enjoy the outdoors — morning, noon, or night; patio to peaks, poolside to lakeside — as you eat.

(OPPOSITE PAGE) *Having the right tools is essential for the barbecuer or camp cook. Almost anything to be cooked can be handled with this array of fork, spatula, brushes, and tongs.*

Tailgating:
The 20th Century
Chuck Wagon

Tailgating at sports events is an activity that makes a parking lot almost homey — sharing food, spirits, sports talk, and recipes. Parking lot feasts may be served on paper, plastic, or china; dished from crockpots, silver platters (for Homecoming, of course), or bandana-lined baskets. Equipment and tools for tailgate picnics can be a mix of *al fresco* and portable grill standards, previously listed, with a sure supply of ice and perhaps a folding table and chairs.

Football games in Arizona have been known to get under way during 100-plus-degree weather. At such times, I expect someone to emulate the picnic that sent the Mole into ecstasy in the classic, *Wind in the Willows*: "cold chicken, cold tongue, cold ham, cold beef, lemonade, ale, and ginger beer." That should do it — with ice, please!

(OPPOSITE PAGE) *The chilly water of an Arizona mountain stream is nature's icebox for cooling canned drinks outdoors. Drag bag and empty cans are carried out afterward, leaving the area clean for future camping.*

Shopping

In a year's research for this book, I was surprised to discover that more than 50 percent of outdoor food is done ahead — munchies, trimmed veggies, appetizers, side dishes, frozen stew, and desserts. Entrees are the on-site stars.

Consider, then, the make-aheads and the take-alongs when food shopping at the supermarket or the camp-outfit emporium. For days or weeks in the wild, factor in such ingredients as nutritional value, weight, ease of preparation, cooking utensils needed, cleanup, and packaging.

In the best tradition of Colin Fletcher, take along "menu-varying goodies" — canned oysters, frog legs, cocktail meatballs, mintcake candies, fudge-rum bars, and a small bottle of claret. On such exotica, Fletcher became the first man in recorded history to walk the length of the Grand Canyon. Of course, he had the usual dried fruit, soup, cereals, and pemmican. You, too, should always have such light, reliable emergency food. Camping outfitter Bill Gilcrest suggests today's interesting goodies:

Bagels
Power bars
Peppered homemade jerky
Pancake mix
Pasta and sauce packets
Olive oil and herbs
Dehydrated tomatoes
Steamer, for fresh vegetables
Pilot crackers
Water and coffee filters
Ghee and Gatorade
Smoked salmon
Cheddar and chocolate in cold weather

Water

Thoreau wrote: "Water has more life in it than any part of the earth's surface." Sadly, elements of the life in it today are threatening. Pure stream water is as rare as the Lost Dutchman's gold. One rule prevails: *Purify all drinking and cooking water found in the back country.*

How? Four common ways are: chlorinating, adding iodine, boiling, and filtering. I've camped with hikers who stay healthy by swishing 2 to 5 drops of chlorine bleach per quart of water in their canteens. The same proportions go for iodine. Common forms of water purification tablets are Potable Aqua (iodine) and Halazone (chlorine). Iodine purifiers are considered most effective, some preferring a 2 percent tincture of iodine. Bleach and iodine must be given time to kill — about an hour.

Boil water hard for 5 minutes. Yes, boiling makes for flat-tasting water (hot, too), but a little lemon juice or salt or a vitamin C tablet improves that.

Primarily, what must be destroyed is *Giardia*, a protozoan that causes chronic diarrhea and cramps and must be treated with prescription drugs. Portable filters are another option. Check your sporting goods store for more information.

Fire

Be sure you obtain a fire permit when necessary, and *read* it. Build fires away from vehicles, tents, and equipment. Check overhanging trees and wind directions before selecting a site. Keep a shovel, a bucket of sand or dirt, and bucket of water handy. Better yet, carry a lightweight stove.

Okay, no big fires. But there are a variety of ways to start small blazes. An inch of steel wool or a slice of a steel cleaning pad will flame with one match. Or, the short, 15-minute emergency highway flares make good fire starters. Or, melt old candle stubs into fiber egg carton sections half-filled with sawdust. Mix, then stick in a piece of heavy cotton cord for a wick.

Want a prettier fire? Pour melted wax over pine cones. Want an appetizing fire? Save leftover cooking grease and pour it on kindling. Use those before the bears smell 'em.

If you brought milk cartons in your cooler, fill them with charcoal; they are dandy, quick fire aids. Getting a fire permit is no guarantee that the fire will start, especially if it rains as you sleep. Gather dry wood before you hit the sack, to cache in a plastic bag or under cover. Make rain an advantage. Put out pots or buckets to gather wash water.

(OPPOSITE PAGE) *A hot dog at home was never like this. Fall foliage colors Hart Prairie in the high country of northern Arizona. One of many ideal spots in the state to pitch a tent, roll out a sleeping bag, fire up a favorite outdoor cooker, and make good food taste great.*

Outdoor Cooking

Clean-up

Aluminum foil is the silver lining of outdoor cooking. Almost anything can be steam-cooked in foil. Then, if you must scrub something, crumple the foil you cooked with, team it with hot water, and presto! Foil cleans grills, too. But pack out the foil, along with the rest of your refuse. If you soap the bottoms of cooking pots, the soot washes right off.

You should have a special grill for cooking fish. One smart camper told me he always takes two simple grills, one for meat and one for finny food, along with a wire brush. Clean grills after every meal, let the residue burn off over the coals, then brush or scour the grill rudely. Standard grills fit in standard grocery store plastic bags.

Clean and Healthy

If you get a common sting — bee, wasp, or mosquito — meat tenderizer eases the pain. If you lose a battle with those tiny, pesky cactus spines, hair remover will dissolve them. Wait 10 minutes and wipe them out and off.

Baby wipes are perfect for quick camping cleanups, and as effective as toothpaste for removing fish odors from hands. Baking soda, lemon juice, or tomato juice will do that, too. And tomato juice is the best friend your dog has if he tangles with a skunk.

(OPPOSITE PAGE) A cooking fire is always at hand with a lightweight backpacker's camp stove. Set it up on a convenient stump or flat rock, away from flammable materials, and a steaming hot meal can be ready in minutes.

Cooking

Whenever you are cooking, precautions are a must. Look for anything that a spark could ignite, from dry leaves to fuel. Keep children and pets at a distance, and be sure somebody is always watching the grill.

In the 30 minutes it takes coals to burn down, assemble the grill tools and anything else you need. With a gas barbecue, the most important point is a quick wipe-off of any grease or wind-blown dust before cooking. Do *not* use your water pistol to extinguish flames at a gas grill. Simply move the food and lower the heat until flaring subsides.

When briquets are glowing, spread out for direct grilling, or arrange around a drip pan for indirect grilling. Use the hand test: Hold your hand, palm side down, above the coals at the height where your food will be cooked. Count seconds — "one thousand one, one thousand two . . ." If you jerk your hand up at two seconds, the coals are hot; after three seconds, they're medium-hot; after four seconds, medium; after six seconds, slow.

Remember the 10-minute tip for fish grilling. Measure at the thickest part, and tuck the tail under for even thickness. Cook 10 minutes for each inch of thickness. Fish is done when translucent becomes opaque and it flakes at the center. Overcooked, fish is dry and tasteless; undercooked, it can make you sick. In most of Arizona, fish and meats should be kept refrigerated until cooking time.

Glossary

Agave - desert plant used for food, drink, and syrup.

Aji-Mirin - Japanese rice sauce.

Ajo - garlic.

Arroz - rice.

Atole - corn gruel.

Barbacoa - Spanish name for early barbecue originated by Caribbean Indians.

Baste - to moisten meat while cooking, using butter or drippings.

Briquet, briquette - refined "pillows" of charcoal, anthracite, peach pits, and other material.

Brisket - meat cut from breast of animal, usually beef.

Buñuelos - sweet, deep-fried fritters.

Burro, burrito - flour tortilla, filled and rolled.

Butter Buds - dried butter-flavor substitute.

Canola oil - oil pressed from canola bean, the current choice of the health conscious.

Carne - meat.

Carne machaca - battered meat seasoned with lime juice and chiles.

Carne seca - dried meat, as jerky.

Carob - breadfruit bean used as chocolate substitute— more nutritious, less chocolate flavor.

Cerveza - beer.

Ceviche - fish marinated in citrus juice and spices until protein is "cooked"; also seviche.

Chia seed - tiny black seed of desert sage; protein source.

Chile - hot pods indigenous to Mexico.

Chileajo - chile and garlic.

Chile con carne - Mexican meat dish with chiles, no beans.

Chili con carne - American version of above; a "bowl of red," often with red or pink beans.

Chile verde - chile dish made with green chiles.

Chimney - safe fire starter, usually made from tin can.

Chitterlings - hog's "innards," fried or boiled, well-seasoned.

Cholla buds - fruit of cholla cactus, somewhat edible.

Chorizo - sausage seasoned with red peppers.

Chuck wagon - kitchen on wheels; "chuck" is the food.

Clambake - fresh clams steam-baked over fire or in coals, usually with lobster and corn; of Indian-New England origin.

Cold cooking - foods either precooked or not requiring fire; preferred by those who like the outdoors more than cooking.

Creosote - desert plant used as tea and medicine.

Cumin - seeds used whole in Mexican dishes and curries, or ground in sauces and entrees.

Cumino - Spanish for the aromatic cumin.

Dry-mop - spices and herbs applied by dry mop or brush on barbecue meat or birds.

Dutch oven - heavy cast-iron pans, best three-legged, with a thick lid; sturdy enough to use in coals.

Fajitas - meat or chicken strips braised with chiles and spices.

Fillet, filet - trimmed steak of fish or meat.

Fire ring - circle or pit enclosed in stone for outside cooking.

Flambé - glazed by liqueur and flame.

Frijoles - beans.

Frito - fried.

Fry bread - Indian bread, patted round and deep-fried; also known as squaw bread and popovers.

Garbanzos - chick-peas.

Gazpacho - cold vegetable soup.

Ghee - liquid butter in tube for camp use.

Glop - mixture of foods remaining at end of trail trip.

Gonch - hook used to lift hot lids from Dutch oven.

Gorp - mixture of nuts, seeds, chocolate, dried fruits, and salty nibbles to chomp on as energy booster.

Granita - coarsely frozen fruit and juice, served as palate cleanser.

Granola - oats, dried fruit bits, coconut, and seeds baked as a high-energy cereal.

Harina - flour.

Hibiscus - dried red and pink flowers of the hibiscus plant, which act as flavor and purifying agents in tea or punch, or in water bottle.

High-impact - visible, environmentally destructive use.

Hominy - whole or ground hulled corn,

processed in a lye bath to remove the germ and plump the kernel.

Humus - garlic-laden puree of chick-peas.

Hush puppies - down-home cornmeal dumplings fried with catfish.

Jalapeño - small, fiery-hot, green pepper.

Javelina - wild peccary.

Jerky - dried meat in strips, highly seasoned.

Jicama - crisp, sweet, white, radish-like Mexican vegetable.

Kabob, kebab, kebob - Far East method of grilling small chunks of meat on stick or skewer, now used also for vegetables and fruits.

Kasha - buckwheat grits.

Lard - rendered fat of hog; the most-used shortening on the frontier, still popular for some Indian and Mexican dishes.

Latkes - in Jewish cooking, thin pancakes of shredded potatoes and vegetables.

Lava rock - volcanic rock which deflects dripping juices and protects heat units of gas and electric grills.

Liquid starter - fluid for starting barbecue fires; ignites quickly; explosive; not to be used after fire is going; leaves unpleasant aftertaste if not allowed to burn off coals before food goes on grill.

Logan bread - dense, heavy bread which keeps for weeks on the trail.

Masa - Corn ground into flour-like mixture, used most often for making tortillas and tamales.

Mesquite - desert plant or tree, used as fuel; now a flavor-enhancer unique to grilling; mesquite beans are an Indian staple.

Mirin - rice wine used in cooking.

Mole - sauce or paste served with meat or fowl, often darkened by cocoa bean or ground chocolate.

Mul-Chu-Tha - Pima Indian annual ceremonial fair.

Nixtamal - hominy.

Nopales - edible pads of prickly pear cactus.

Nouvelle grill - latest and trendiest grill foods and techniques.

Nutritionally dense - lacking chemicals or preservatives, but with plenty of food value per ounce.

One-liners - simple recipes for the trail.

One-pot meals - stews, crockpot mixes, glop, and Dutch oven delights.

Opuntia - prickly pear cactus.

Paella - seafood and chicken dish of Spanish origin.

Pepitas - inner kernel of pumpkin seed.

Pesto - fresh herb sauce, most often basil.

Pie irons - circles of metal on handles, for over-fire cooking.

Piki - Hopi blue-corn bread, crisp and thin as paper.

Pinto bean - freckled bean, Arizona's favorite.

Pipikalua - tasty Hawaiian spiced jerky.

Posole - stew of pork and corn.

Quelites - wild spring greens; also called purslane.

Salsa cruda - uncooked hot sauce.

Salsa de chile verde - green chile sauce.

Scone - muffin cooked on griddle, originally Scottish oats.

Shoyu - soy sauce.

Smoker - cooking methods including cold smoking (low temperature over a long period of time), water smoking (pan of water or wine under food creates a smoky fog), and hot smoking (wood or chips added to coals).

S'mores - traditional camping dessert of chocolate and marshmallow melted over the fire on a graham cracker.

Squeeze cheese - soft cheese in a squeeze tube.

Stuff sacks - water-resistant sacks, ideally nylon, for keeping culinary items and other gear separated but available.

Taco - crisp corn shell with stuffing; word means "wad."

Tepary bean - small, power-packed, wild bean of the desert.

Tequila - volcanic Mexican drink distilled from the fermented agave plant.

Tomari - natural soy sauce preferred by natural-food cooks.

Tortilla - thin, flat, griddle-baked bread made from either corn or wheat flour.

Wheat germ - outer bran of grain.

Wood chips - chips of apple, oak, mesquite, or other aromatic hardwoods tossed on coals to add wood-smoke flavor to grilled food.

Zappers - quick wet and dry mops for adding fire and spice to grilled meats.

Index

Editor's Note: Page numbers in bold face indicate recipes. Page numbers followed by letter p (56p) indicate photos.

A

Abiding Savior Lutheran
   Church, 140
Adams, Alvan, 25
Adams Hotel, 131
*Adventures of Tom Sawyer,
   The*, 45
Aioli Sauce, **89**
Ajo, Ariz., 64
Albert's Pesto Supreme, **84**
All-day Cup, **128**
Allen Leg of Lamb, **34**
Allen, Phil, 34
Allen, Rex, 12
Allingham, Ginger, 114
All-purpose Salsa, **18**
Allyn, Mrs. James S., 21
American Egg Board, 15
American Institute
   for Cancer Research, 149
American Institute of Wine
   and Food, 113
Anaheim chiles, 65p
Anchor and Editor Lamb, **34**
Andlauer, Carol and Fred, 44
An Ounce of Prevention, 149
Antelope, **36**
Apache Indians, 95
Apache Reservation, 131
Apples, 70, **73**, 75, 118
Apricot-mustard Sauce, **91**
Apricots, 75, 76, 118
Arizona Club, 52
Arizona Cowbelles, 138
Arizona Federation
   of Garden Clubs, 24
Arizona Game and Fish
   Department, 40
Arizona Highways, 15
*Arizona Highways
   Heritage Cookbook*, 16, 132
Arizona Historical Society,
   85, 111
Arizona National Livestock
   Show, 30
*Arizona Queen Fish,
   Unlimited*, **44**
Arizona Republic, The, 89
Arizona State University,
   47, 85, 141
Arizona State University
   Experimental Farm, 38
Arizona Sun Tea, **124**,
*Arizona Territorial Cookbook,
   The*, 37, 138
Arleen's Swedish Fruit Zoop, **131**
Arugula, 61p
Ash bread, 95

Asian Omelet, **17**
Atoles, 120, **127**
Avocado Blend, **87**
Avra Valley, Ariz., 148

B

Babbitt, Bruce, 12
Backpacker's Pizza, **146**, 147p
Backpacking, 156-157, 161
Backyard Ironed
   Pita Pockets, **140**
Bananas, 70, **74, 75,** 76
Bananas in Blankets, **74**
Barbecue, 6, 7, 28, **30, 31, 32,**
   33p, **34, 35, 36, 37, 38, 39,
   40, 41,** 80, 81, 82, 87, **88, 89**
Barbecue Sauces, 78, **80, 81, 82,
   84, 87, 88, 89**
Barger, Sharon, 81
Bartram, Petie and Ray, 98
Basic Chile Sauce, **82**
Basil Vinaigrette, **49**
Baynham, Owen, 143
Bean Ball, Incredible, **146**
Bean Bread, **102**
Bean Dogs, **138**
Bean Salad, **68, 149**
Bean Sprout Omelet, **16**
Beans, 60, **64, 68, 146, 149**
Beard, James, 36
Beef, 28, **30, 31, 32,** 33p, **35,
   36,** 36p, **37, 38, 39, 41,** 53p,
   80p, **152**
Beef ribs, 80p
Beeler, Joe, 19
Beer in cooking, 153
Bell peppers, 62
Bell, Rabbi Maynard, 63
Benson, Ariz., 81
Bentzin-Torbert, Dorothy, 135
Berries, 70, 75, 76, 118
Berry, John, 151
Beverages, 120-135
Beverly, Molly, 66
Big Tiny Little's Broccoli
   Crunch, **69**
Billie Jo's Poolside Salad, **69**
Birchermuesli, **25**
Biscooks, **97**
Biscuits, 96, 96p, **97, 146**
Biscuits on a Stick, **97,** 97p
Bishop, Bob, 134
Bish's Cappuccino, **134**
Black Bean & Pepper
   Pleasure, **149**
Black River, Ariz., 43p, 155p
Blake, Cliff, 157
Blatt, Erna, 100
Bloody Mary, **26**
Blue Corn Chile Bread, **98,** 99p
Blushing Bunny, **130**
Bogota Bread Omelet, **15**
Bombeck, Erma, 12
Bonanza Bread, **101**

Bonnie's Buffalo Steak, **40**
Boy Scouts, 4, 157
Bradshaw Mountains, 64
Brass, Laura, 8
Braunbeck, Orval, 81
Breads, 6, 7, 92-105
Breakfast, 12-27, 13p
Breakfast on a Stick, **27,** 27p
Brenna's Chile con Queso
   Dunk, **147**
Brenner, George, 44
Bright, Bobbie, 38
Broccoli, **69,** 69p
Brock, Pat, 126
Brooks, Joyce and Brenna, 147
Brown, Bud and Isabelle, 96
Brown, James Carrington
   "Bing", 118
Brunette Pears, **119**
Budget Bender Hot
   Chocolate Mix, **126**
Buffalo, 28, **40**
Buler, Bob and Claire, 32
Bullion, Mrs. Homer L., 66
Burrito Burgers, **139**

C

Caballero, Ramon, 84
Cabrillo, 45
Callahan, Pat, 111
Camelback Mountain, 88
Campaign Creek, 157p
Camp Biscuits with Daisies, **97**
Camp Bread, **105**
Camp Cappuccino, **134**
Camp Coffee to Suit 'em All, **22**
Campfire Boys and Girls, 4, 157
Camping, 154-167, 155p, 157p,
   159p, 165p
Camp Verde, Ariz., 108
Candelaria, Frank, 52
Candelaria Picnic Chicken, **52**
Cappuccino, **134**
Carefree, Ariz., 87, 143
Carlisle, Sid, 32
Carne Machaca, **16**
Carob Coconut Cookies, **114**
Caroler's Wassail Bowl, The, **135**
Carrington Fresh Picked
   Cobbler, **118**
Carrots, 63p, 69p
Carter, Roseanne and Marsha, 94
Cartwright School District, 23
Cartwright, Shirley
   and Charles, 23
Catfish, 47
Catholic Overseas Mission, 32
Cauliflower, 69p
Cave Creek, Ariz., 57, 109
Chandler, Ariz., 55
Charcoal, 8
Checklists: Fuel & Tools, 11;
   Trail, 156; Picnic, 158;

Camping, 163
Cheesy Biscuits, **146**
Cheesy Lambburgers, **36**
Cherries, 70, 118
Cherry Ham Glaze, **88**
Chia seeds, 152
Chicken, **50, 51, 52,** 54p, **55,
   58p, 59, 85**
Chigger Flats Scramble, **15**
Child, Julia, 15, 28
Chileajo Vegetables, **66**
Chiles, 65p
Chile Sauce, **82**
Chili, White, 58p, **59**
Chill Factor Avocado Blend, **87**
Chill Quenchers, **129**
Chino Valley, Ariz., 66
Chocolate Pancakes, **20**
Chocolate Turtle
   Cheesecake, 110p, **111**
Chris's Yogurt Serve, **129**
Christopher's Red Wine
   Prime, **31**
Chuck wagon, 6, 29p, 158, 163
Chuck Wagon Cookin', 138
Church, Hades, 22
Civil War Cake, **108**
Clambake, **47**
Clark, Vikki, 36
Claxton, Sue Mitchell, 141
Clean-up, 167
Clements, Karen, 126
Cochran, Mary L., 24
Cocoa, 120
Coffee, 22,26, 120
Coffee Can Bread, **100**
Coffee Cookies, **116**
Colleary, Barbara and Jim, 47
Colorado River, 143
Conte, Lucia, 64
Cookie Tacos, **113,** 113p
Cookies for Breakfast, **141**
Cooking tips, 2, 167
Cooney, Joan Ganz, 96
Corn, 60, 62, **67,** 67p
Corn Relish, 68p
Covey, Mitzie and Richard, 31
Cowbelle Pan Cakes, **21**
Cowboy Artists of America,
   19, 20
Cow Country Cuisine, 16
Crazy, Mixed-up Popcorn, **153**
Crew's Sunshine Cooler,
   The, **124**
Crockpot Posole, **38**
Cropp, Mildred, 82
Cullumber, Sue, 146
Cup o' Kindness, **26**

D

Daisy Mountain Volunteer Fire
   Department Auxiliary, 36
Date Loaf, **112**
Davis, Carolyn, 101

de Alba, Felipe, 132
De Grazia, Ted, 152
Desert Botanical Garden, 105, 123
Desert, Down East Clambake, **47**
Desert Jade Junior Women's Club, 85
Desserts, 106-119
Devlin, Vincent and Emily, 18
Devor, Nancy, 14
DeWald, Scott, 142
DeWald, Terry and Peggy, 101
Diane's Vegetable Squares, **148**
Dirt, **117**
Doctor Mom's Luscious Lemonade, **124**, 125p
Dog Kabobs, **138**
Donavon, Billie Jo, 69
Don's Mustard Sauce, **88**
Dorothee's Kahlúa Kabobs, **89**
Dottie's AZ-Tex Barbecue Best, **82**
Dove, 51, **57**
Dried Apples, **73**
Dried Ground Beef Mix, **152**
Drinkwater, Herb, 35
Dryer, John, 41
Dunkin' Platters, **117**
Dutch oven, 11, 35, 37, 38, 39, 40, 41, 59, 64, 67p, 92, 94, 96, 96p, 118, 136, 138, 140, 151, 158
Dutch Oven Biscuits, **96**, 96p

E

Eagle Scout Date Loaf, **112**
Earle's Prickly Pear Punch, **123**
Earle, W. Hubert and Lucille, 123
Ease-it, Spice-it Tuna Grill, **46**
Easiest-ever Hollandaise, **91**
Eggplant, 62, 63p
Eggs, **14, 15, 16, 17**
Eisenhower, Dwight, 17
Elfrida, Ariz., 148
Elgin, Ariz., 45
Elin's Hunan Lamb Salad, **34**
Elk, **36**, 41
Elsie's Fish Sauce, **85**
Embery, Dottie, 82
Embery, Pam Rhoads and Richard, 45, 82, 174p
Encanto Park, 88, 158
Enchantment Granola, **24**, 157
Escabeche, **45**
Evert, Chris, 129
Everybody's Hawaiian Chicken, **55**
Everything But the Ants, 17
Ewald, Ellen Buchman, 127
Eye-opener One, **26**

F

Faris, Betty Jean, 16
Fenzl, Barbara and Terry, 113
Fenzl Fancy Cookie Tacos, **113**, 113p
Fickeisen, Norm and Flo, 143
1500s, **114**, 115p
Finch, Jan and Dan, 30, 36
Fires, 8-11, 164
First Families of Arizona, 105
Fish, 42, **44, 45, 46, 47, 49, 50**
Fish Sauce, **85**
Five-bean Salad, **66**
Flagstaff, Ariz., 97, 148
Flagstaff Methodist Church, 97
Fletcher, Colin, 83, 163
Foiled Breakfast, **14**
Foil pot cooking, 14
Forest Service, U.S., 131, 157
Fort Huachuca, Ariz., 128
Foster, Helen, 15
Fowl, 42, **50, 51, 52, 55, 56, 57, 59**
Franz, Carl, 146
French Fries, **62**
French Toast, **22**, 98
Friedland, Harriet, 50
Friendly Pines Camp, 96
Friends of Rehab, 148
Frosted Root Beer, **127**
Frozen Fruit Yogurt, **76**
Fruit Cobbler, **118**
Fruited Amaretto Sauce, **90**, 90p
Fruit Kabobs, **133**
Fruit Leather, **75**
Fruit 'n' Nut Crust, **117**
Fruits, 70-77, 71p
Fruit Sorbet, **76**, 77p
Fry bread, 92, 93p, 94, **95**
Fuels & Tools, 11
Fuller, Ross, 96
Funnel Cakes, **21**

G

Galletas de Cafe, **116**
Gallons of Garbanzos Salad, **66**
Game, 24,28, 39,**40**, 41
Garbanzo beans, 66
Gary's Game Meat Sausage, **24**
George Brenner's Basic Trout, **44**
George, Mrs. Dick, 117
George, G.G., 112
German Pancakes, **20**
Giffis, B.J., 117
Gila Bend, Ariz., 148
Ginger Ice Cream, **117**
Girl Scouts, 4, 8, 157
Glendale, Ariz., 148
Glendale Gauchos, 114
Globe, Ariz., 16, 52
Go Bananas on the Grill, **74**
Golden, Ferol Smith, 56

Gonzales, Jose, 64
Goober Dogs, **138**
Good Samaritan Hospital, 148
Gordon, Kathy and Bruce, 50
Gorman, Marion, 132
Gorp, **142**, 142p
Gorp, Glop, & Glue Stew, 24
Graham, Marlinda, 67
Grandad's Scratch Biscuits, **96**, 96p
Grand Canyon, 22, 83, 108, 142, 163
Grand Canyon White Sauce, **83**
Grandfather Gonzales' Beans, **64**
Grandfather Nebeker's Pancakes, **20**
Granita, **76**
Granola, **24**, 140, 157
Gravy, **141**
Great Bean Sprout Omelet, **16**
Green beans, 66
Green Chile Escalloped Potatoes, **23**
Green Chile Wineburger, **36**
Griffen, Bert and Elizabeth, 112
Grilled Game Hens with Jalapeño Glaze, **56**
Grilled Ham and New Potatoes, **23**
Grilled Martini Salmon, **49**
Grilled Salmon Salad, **49**
Grills, 10, 11
Grits in a Ring, **25**
Greenhouse Mesquite Muffins, **105**
Greenhouse, Ruth, 105
Gross, Christopher, 31
Guero chiles, 65p
Gwen's Las Madrinas Marinade, **82**

H

Hackett House, 47
Halibut, **46**
Ham, **23, 35, 39**, 88
Hamburgers, **36**, 36p, 137p
Hampton, John, 19
Happy Valley Hot Flash, **143**
Harding, Don, 88
Harer, Albert E. Sr., 105
Harriet's Paella Salad, **50**
Hartneck, Mary Jane, 35
Hart Prairie, 159p, 165p
Hayden Mill, 148
Heard Museum, 148
Heminghaus, Arleen, 131
Hennessey, George, 131
Herbert, A.P., 25
Hernandez, Barbara, 95
Hibiscus Tea, 120, **123**
Hibiscus Tea Punch, 121p, 122p, **123**
High, Mary and Roy, 47
Hiking, 157

Hirsch, Mary and Bob, 39, 57, 109
Holbrook, Ray and Sheri, 16
Hollandaise Sauce, **91**
Holy Family Retreat Association, 14
Homemade Instant Breakfast, **127**
Hominy Grits, **25**
Honey Sweetener, **124**
Hooper, Mildred, 116
Hopi Cookery, 128
Hopi Indians, 67, 98, 128, 149
Hopi Milk Drink, **128**
Hopi Pit-baked Corn, **67**
Hot Buttered Cider, **135**
Hot Chocolate Mix, **126**
Hot Dogs, **138**, 138p
Houseboating, 145p
Hubbell, Alberta, 100
Huevos Rancheros, **14**
Hughes, Stella, 138

I

Incredible Bean Ball, The, **146**
Instantly Breakfast, **24**
International Holistic Center, 117
Italian Barbecue Baste, **81**
Italian Bread on the Barbecue, **94**
Iwai, Stan, 85

J

Javelina, 41
Jeffords, Elin, 34
Jelks' Basic Beach Menu, **45**
Jelks, Keri and Ruki, 45
Jeri's Lime-time Hens, **51**
Jerome, Ariz., 127
J & J Gorp, **142**, 142p
John's Beerchuck, **41**
John's Green Chile Wineburger, **36**
Johnson, Connie, 64
Joyce's Chicken-fried Venison, **40**
Juice-sicles, **76**
Juicy Lucies, **36**

K

Kabobs, **52**, 53p, **62**, 80, **89, 133, 138**
Kahlúa Dreamer, **135**
Kavena, Juanita Tiger, 128, 149
Kazuko Fish Teriyaki, **46**
Keams Canyon, Ariz., 148
Kell, Dee, 114
Kelling, Kathie, 68
Kelling Red Onion Salad, **68**
Kelson, Stan, 117
Kennedy, Beth, 18
Kennedy-Iwai, Ruth Ann, 18

Index

Kennedy, John F., 39
Kettle Cantaloupe Birds, **51**
Kidney beans, 66
Kimble, Socorro Munoz, 116
King, Frank, 135
Kissinger, Dottie and John, 80
Kitts, Sonny, 128
Kiwi, 71p
Kline, Irene, 148
Korean-style Barbecued Meat, 32
Kraus, Barbara, 62

L

Lacy, Susan, 15
Lake Montezuma, Ariz., 112
Lake Powell, 145p
Lakes Cookbook, 124
Lakes, The, 124
Lakeside, Ariz., 26, 98
Lamb, **34, 36,** 53p, **152**
Lambburgers, Cheesy, **36**
Latkes, **63**
Laveen, Ariz., 32
Laveen Barbecue, **32,** 33p
Laveen Lions Club, 32
Leftover Blessing, **77**
Lemonade, 120, 121p, **124,** 125p
Lemon Loaf, **112**
Lemon Tarts, 107p
Les Gourmettes
   Cooking School, 113
Let 'em Eat Dirt, **117**
Lima beans, 66
Lindley, Irene, 19
Lipinski, Bessie, 127
Little, Big Tiny and Nancy, 69
Logan bread, 92, **100**
London Broil Mexican, **30**
Lost Dutchman Gold Mine, 73
Love for Three Oranges, **72**
Lucia's Verdolagas, **64**
Lucille's Tupe Sauce
   Marinade, **80**
Luscious Lemonade, 121p,
   124, 125p
Luscious Lemon Loaf, **112**

M

MacArthur, Douglas, 17
Machaca and Eggs, **16**
Mackerel, **46**
Maple Syrup Banana Cake, **74**
Margarita, **132**
Maricopa County Extension
   Service, 95
Marinades, **30, 31, 32,**
   34, 35, 78-91
Marks, Marty, 52
Mason, Helen, 130
Massachusetts Institute
   of Technology, 119
Masse, Peter, 94

Matsui, Nancy and Clyde, 55
Mau, Jane, 22
Maui, 80
Mayor Drinkwater's Special, **35**
McCleve, Michael, 88
McCleve's Steel Etcher Salsa, **88**
McMahon, Pat, 12
McRaine, Kathy, 16
Meat, 28-41
Meissner, Bill and Gail, 116
Mesa, Ariz., 46, 55, 80, 94, 151
Mescal, 151
Mesquite Muffins, **105**
Mexican Desserts, 116
Mexican-French Toast, **22,** 22p
Meyers, DeDe, 91
Michlipsy, Lee, 151
Mogollon Rim, 84
Mole-in-the-Hole, **15**
Molly's Chileajo Vegetables, **66**
Monument Valley, Ariz., 109
Morgan, Kay and Joseph, 46
Most Three-in-one Roast, **39**
Mul-Chu-Tha, 95
Mummy Mountain, 18
Mushroom Comfort Sauce, **87**
Mushrooms, 62, 87
Mustard Sauce, **88**
Myers, Pat, 142

N

Nachos, 150p, **151**
Nasser, Diane, 148
National Association of
   Cowbelles, 80
National Hot Dog
   and Sausage Council, 138
Nature's Kitchen, 76
Navajo Sprout Cake, **109**
Navajo Taco, 93p, **148**
Navajo Tribal Fair, 95
Nebeker, Merry and Bill, 20
Nemmers, Gwen and Keith, 82
New Cornelia Mine, 64
New River, Ariz., 40
Nielson, Mrs. Lars, 117
Niemiec, Annie and Frank, 91
Niethammer, Carolyn, 146
Noah's Ark Chowder, **130,** 130p
Noble, Catherine, 59
No-fail Fiesta Cake, **109**
Nopales Mexapil, **64**
Noriega, Irma Serrano, 116
Northern Arizona Pioneers
   Historical Society, 66
Nouvelle grill, 60
"Now You've Got It, What Are
   You Gonna Do With It?", 39

O

Olais, Gus and Ophelia, 64
Olé Turkey Mole, **84**

Omelets, **15, 16, 17**
Onions, 62
On-Off-the-Road Cookbook, 146
Opuntia, 64
Orange Chocolate Chip Muffins,
   102, 103p
Orange-Ginger Chicken, **51**
Orange Julie, 121p, **129**
Oranges, **72**
Outpost Coffee, **26**
Outreach Stew, **148**
Oyster Chile Sauce, **85**
Oyster Sauce, **85**
Oyster Sauce Chicken, **85**

P

Packing tips, 161
Paella Salad, **50**
Painted Pears, **75**
Palmer, Nancy, 102
Pancake Dividends, **21**
Pancakes, **18, 19,** 19p, **20, 21**
Pann, Lori and Bart, 74
Paradise Valley, Ariz., 15, 18, 63
Paria Canyon, Ariz., 151
Paria Nachos, 150p, **151**
Pasta Sauce, **35**
Patio Pseudo Fillet, **31**
Patio Sauce, **62**
Pat's Arizona Chocolate
   Turtle Cheesecake, 110p, **111**
Pat's Ski Tea, **126**
Peaches, **72, 75, 76,** 118
Peach Soup, **72,** 72p
Peachy Lime Granita, **76**
Peanut Butter Pancake
   Prerun Breakfast, **18**
Peanuts, 153
"Peanuts," 21
Pears, 70, **75,** 119
Peg's Scalloped Pineapple, **77**
Peg's Whole Wheat Getcha-
   there-and-back Rolls, **101**
Pemberton, Luella, 41
Peoria, Ariz., 116
Pepitas, 152
Peplow, Bonnie and Ed, 138
Peralta Apples, **73**
Peralta, Pedro, 73
Pesto Sauce, **84**
Phillips, Gov. John C., 141
Phoenix, Ariz., 21, 31, 34, 36, 52,
   55, 57, 67, 73, 74, 81, 85, 88,
   117, 123, 126, 129, 131, 139,
   141, 148, 151, 158
Phoenix Baptist Hospital
   Auxiliary, 82
Phoenix Home & Garden, 113
Phoenix Junior League, 17
Phoenix Racquets, 129
Phoenix Suns, 25
Picnickers Checklist, 158
Picnics, 158, 161
Pie irons, 10p, 139, 139p

Pierson, Lisa, 17
Pillsbury Bake-off, 95
Pima Indians, 95, 118
Pineapple, 71p, **72, 75, 77, 134**
Pineapple-Banana Sherbet, **75**
Pineapple Bolo, **134**
Pineapple Pleasure, **72**
Pine, Ariz., 41, 84, 96, 100
Pineda, Rudy, 14
Pine-Strawberry
   Homemakers Club, 100
Piñon nuts, **149**
Pinto Beans, **64**
Pioneer Stockman's Association,
   94
Pita Pockets, **140**
Pita Wedges, **130**
Pizza, 92
*Pleasant Valley Homemakers
   Cookbook*, 19, 97
Plums, 75
Polson, Dorothee, 89
Pompano, **45**
Pon (Camp Bread), **105**
Poole, Barbara Louise, 49
Poolside Mexican-French
   Toast, **22,** 22p
Popcorn, 152p, **153**
Popovers, Indian, 95, 93p
Popper French Fries, **62**
Poppy Seed Dressing, **69**
Pork, 28, **38**
Posole, **38**
Potatoes, **23,** 60, **62,** 83p
Pot Roast, **38**
Poultry Insurance Policy, 51
Powdered Milk, 128
Prater and Mendenhall, 24
Pre-breakfast Jolts, **26**
Prescott, Ariz., 20, 37, 96, 140
Prickly pear cactus, 64
Prickly Pear Punch, 121p, **123**
Pul Kogi, 32
Pumpkin Carrot Coffee
   Cake, **111**
Pumpkin seeds, 152
Punches, 133
Punkin Center, Ariz., 41
Purple Sage and Other Pleasures, 62
Purslane, **64**

Q

Quail, **51, 56**
Quail in Hot Ashes, **56**
Queen Creek, Ariz., 21
Quick Chicken Kabobs, **52**
Quick Chill Quenchers, **129**

R

Radicchio, 61p
Radishes, 69p
Randel, John, 32

Raspberry Dipped Fruit, **116**
Ray's No-frill Grill, **30**
Recipe Roundup, 105
*Recipes from Arizona,
    with Love*, 56
Red Chile Sauce, 78
Red Eye Gravy, **141**
Red Mountain, 7p
Red Onion Salad, **68**
REI, 146
Reid, Frank, 97
Renwick, Ethel Hulbert, 87
Rhodes, Congressman
    and Mrs. John J., 38
Rhodes Hot Salsa Pot Roast, **38**
Rhum Coconut Sauce, **91**
Ribs, 35
Ribs, Sausage, and Ham, **35**
Riemersma, Mary, 139
Roasting Ears, **67**
Rob's Mexican Spa Chicken, **55**
Rockfish, **46**
Rodier, Grace B., 17
Rodriguez, Dr. Roy, 16
Roundup Recipes, 138
Ruffner, Budge, Elisabeth,
    Melissa, 37, 138
Ruffner Dutch-oven Roast, **37**
Rukkila, Joyce and Jean, 142
Rukkila, Vi, 59
Ruth's Dressing, **68**
RVs, 158, 159p, 161

S

Sacaton, Ariz., 95
Saguaro Fruit Sundaes, **118**
Saguaro Lake Guest Ranch, 80
Saguaro Lake Ranch
    Barbecue, **80**
Salmon, 48p, **49**
Salsa, **18**, 78, 79p, **88**
Salsa cruda, **18**, 78, 86p
Salsa de Chili Verde, **45**
Salt River, 80
Salt River Valley, 131
Sangria, 120, 121p, **133**
Sangrita (Widow Sanchez
    Style), **132**
San Juan Chicken Curry, **50**
Saraceno, Al
    and Jimmie Ruth, 84
Sardinera del Playa, **45**
Sasabe, Ariz., 148
Sauce for Roasted
    Meats (Indian), **87**
Sauces, 78-91
Sauce the Onions, **83**
Sausage, **24, 35**
Scharf, Daniel, 148
Schneider, Gary and Jeannie, 24
Schranck, Bob, 56
Schultz, Charles, 21
Schwada, John and Wilma, 141
Scottsdale, Ariz., 15, 17, 24, 35,

52, 68, 82
Scripps Institute
    of Oceanography, 84
Sells, Ariz., 95
Seminoff, Dick and Caren, 134
Sesame Street, 96
Shadow Valley Ranch, 140
Shelor, Sheila, 21, 90
Sherbets, 76
Shoofly Cake, **108**
Shopping checklist, 163
Shoyu, 78
Shrimp, **50**, 53p
Sierra Club, 59
Sierra Club Pocket Food Book, 75
Sierra fish, **45**
Simple Foods for the Pack, 59
Sizer, Bill and Bonnie, 39, 40
Skillet Navajo Taco, **148**
Sky Ranch, 66
Smith, Dorothy, 63
Smith, Joy, 68
Sorbet, **76**, 77p
Soups, 120, **130-131**
Sourdough Hot Cakes for 50, **19**
South Mountain Park, 158
South Mountains, 73
Southwest Regional
    Outreach Services, 148
Spaghetti Sauce, **35**
Spartan "Secret"
    Barbecue Sauce, **81**
Spiced Mocha Mix, **126**
Spiced, Smoked Turkey, **57**
Spinach, 61p
Spirits in cooking, 153
Springer, Rob, 55
Springer, Sherri, 94
Sprouts, Bean and Alfalfa, **143**
Squash, 63p
Squaw Bread, 93p
Squaw Peak, 123
Stanfield, Ariz., 148
Stick Apples, **73**
Stilwell, "Vinegar Joe," 17
Stir Fries, **146**
Stone, Mrs. Floyd, 80
Strawberries, 71p
Strawberry, Ariz., 100, 117
Strawberry Plop Sangria,
    121p, **133**
Stuffed French Toast, **98**
Sullivan, Kelley, 108
Summer Spa Soup, **130**
Sunflower seeds, 153
Sunflower Taquitos, **41**
Sunrise Brunch Strata, **17**
Sunset, 94
Sun Tea, 120, **124**,
Superstition Mountains, 73
Sydnor, Dot, 88

T

Tafur, Clemencia and Mario, 15

Tailgating, 163
Tang, Janie, 85
Tart, No-catsup Barbecue
    Sauce, **81**
Tempe, Ariz., 102, 124, 148
Temple Solel, 63
Tepary beans, 146
Tequila Book, The, 132
Teriyaki Chicken Matsui, 54p, **55**
Tewksbury-Graham Feud, 19
Thomas, Vicki and Tom, 57
Tiger's Milk, 127
Tipton, Peg, 41
T.J.'s Sinful Treats, **140**
Tohono O'odham Indians, 95,
    118, 146
Tomatoes Rockefeller, **63**
Tonto Basin, Ariz., 41
Tonto Cowbelles, 41
Tonto National Forest, 157p
Tools (Fuels &), 11, 160p
Topped-out Popcorn, **153**
Tortilla Flats, **45**
Tortillas, 92, **95**
Totem Pole Potatoes, **62**
Trail check list, 156
Trail Mix Bean Salad, **68**
Traveling Fruit Cakes, **116**
Trout, 43p, **44**, 44p
Tucson, Ariz., 16, 56, 62,
    85, 101, 148
Tumbleweed Gourmet, 146
Tuna, **46**
Turkey, **57, 84**
Turkey Mole, **84**
Twain, Mark, 45

U

Udall, Stewart L., 39
University of Arizona, 16, 64, 95
U.S. Forest Service, 131, 157

V

Van Eenemaan, Joanne
    and John, 36
Vannucci, Putsee, 81
Vaughn, Jean, 97
Veal, **39**
Vegetable Kabobs
    with Patio Sauce, **62**
Vegetables, 60-69,61p, 62p, 63p,
    65p, 67p, 68p, 69p
Veggie Latkes, **63**
Venison, 28, **36, 40, 41**
Verdolagas, **64**
Vida, Ray, 30

Vincent, Joyce, 40
Vino Marinade, **30**

W

Wadsworth, Kimer, 129
Waldrip, Evelyn, 126
Wassail Bowl, **135**
Water, purifying, 164
Watson, Tom, 19
Wax beans, 66
Webb Winery, 148
Westerners, The, 111
West, Mary Jo, 55
Wheat Flour Tortilla Mix, **95**
Whiskey Pancakes, **19**
Whitaker and Flournoy, 76
White Chili, 58p, **59**
White Mountains, 14
White Sauce, **83**
Wild in the Kitchen, 56
Willcox, Ariz., 148
Williams, Bill, 157
Willson, Roscoe, 22, 131
Wind in the Willows, 163
Window Rock, Ariz., 95
Wine in cooking, 153
Wise, Anabel, 140
Wise Barbecue for 75, **140**
World of Good Cooking, A, 87

Y

Yogurt, Frozen Fruit, **76**
Young, Ariz., 126
Young, Shirley and Bill, 141
Yuma, Ariz., 111, 148

Z

Zucchini, 62, 63p

Acknowledgments

Many thanks to so many contributors whose names are embedded in the text as well as the index. My gratitude always to each. Loving thanks, too, to my parents and all the fresh-air family members who never cook or eat inside if they can be out — picnic people close to my heart.

Appreciation, too, to those who gave assistance from the Arizona State Parks Department, Arizona Game and Fish Department, Arizona Beef Council, Arizona Cowbelles, the Arizona Historical Society, Arizona Lamb Council, Arizona River Runners, the Arizona Office of Tourism, Boy Scouts of Arizona, Commission on the Arizona Environment, Cowboy Artists of America, Daisy Mountain Fire Department Auxiliary, Encanto Neighborhood Cookbook, First Families of Arizona, Maricopa County Parks and Recreation Department, Paul Schatt, who edited the *Arizona Magazine*, Maricopa County Extension Service, Northern Arizona University School of Hospitality, Phoenix Junior League, Payson Lioness Club, Phoenix Parks Commission, Pleasant Valley Homemakers, Desert Botanical Garden of Phoenix, Tucson Junior League, Tucson Stirring Spoon, Scottsdale Recreation Department, and the U.S. Forest Service.

Alas, there's never quite enough space for even the best. So, for delectable dishes that, regrettably, must wait for another book, thanks to the creators of Terry Wilhoit's Tailgate Chicken, Sue Ellen Allen's Oak Creek Picnic, Hawkins' Great American Luau, Owen Baynham's River Breakfast, Richard Haught's Old Time Camp Cooking, Chuck Brown's San Juan Chili Grit, Solomon's Soul Picnic, Indian Harvest Thanksgiving, Len Huck's Christmas Steak Brunch, Mary Duncan's Dutch Oven Banquet, and Madge Griswold's Shrimp and Snail-Butter Grill.

For sharing beyond the call of duty, thanks to outdoor cooks Ben Avery, Phil Allen, Kit and Bob Applegate, George and Katie Brenner, Bud Brown, Barbara Colleary, Donald Carlson, Sue Cullumber, the Charles Cartwrights, Carolyn Davis, Peggy, Scott, and Terry DeWald, Barb Fenzl, Harriet Friedland, Barbara Gast, Andy Householder, Roy and Mary High, Bob and Mary Hirsch, Mary Jane Hartneck, Stella Hughes, Mildred Hooper, Rukie and Keri Jelks, Elin Jeffords, Connie Johnson, Peg and Don Koch, Dee Kell, Juanita Tiger Kavena, Diana Kessler, Nancy Kelly, Diane Lane, Jane and Herb Metzger, Nancy Matsui, Francie Mallery, Pat Myers, Marguerite Noble, Carolyn Niethammer, Bonnie Peplow, Dorothee Polson, the folks at REI, Eleanor Richardson, Helen Shackelford, Maggie, Tom, and Vikki Thomas, Joyce Vincent, Sara Winter, Paula Jansen, Pete Cowgill, and Steve Stern.

Photographer Richard Embery and food stylist Pam Rhoads Embery had the generous assistance of many as they created the color photography. Their thanks, and ours, go to: Dick Kemp of ARA Leisure Services; Roger Sorenson, Arizona Game and Fish Department; Clovis Sturgeon, Silvercreek Fish Hatchery; Mr. and Mrs. Armand Zildjian; fry bread magician Kay Linda Owens; Sid Carlisle, Laveen Barbecue; Barbara Colleary, Perla Wicks, Mr. and Mrs. H. S. Rhoads, Christine Smith, Mr. and Mrs. Dennis Johnson, Mr. and Mrs. Alan Karns, Mark Allen Embery, and David Elms.

(OPPOSITE PAGE) *Photographer Richard Embery and food stylist Pamela Rhoads Embery prepare the ingredients for a colorful scene illustrating Outdoor Cooking.*